W9-BON-009

TRIANGLE SHIRTWAIST FACTORY FIRE

TRIANGLE SHIRTWAIST FACTORY FIRE

Donna Getzinger

MORGAN REYNOLDS

PUBLISHING

Greensboro, North Carolina

american workers

TRIANGLE SHIRTWAIST FACTORY FIRE

Copyright © 2009 by Donna Getzinger

All rights reserved.
This book, or parts thereof, may not be reproduced in any form
except by written consent of the publisher. For more information write:
Morgan Reynolds Publishing, Inc., 620 South Elm Street, Suite 223
Greensboro, North Carolina 27406 USA

Library of Congress Cataloging-in-Publication Data

Getzinger, Donna.
    The Triangle Shirtwaist Factory fire / by Donna Getzinger.
        p. cm.
    Includes bibliographical references and index.
    ISBN-13: 978-1-59935-099-8 (alk. paper)
    ISBN-10: 1-59935-099-8 (alk. paper)
    1. Triangle Shirtwaist Company--Fire, 1911. 2. Fires--New York (State)--
New York--History--20th century. 3. New York (N.Y.)--History--1898-1951. 4.
Clothing factories--New York (State)--New York--Safety measures--History-
-20th century. 5. Labor laws and legislation--New York (State)--New York--
History--20th century. I. Title.
    F128.5.G48 2008
    974.7'1041--dc22

                                                    2008004077

Printed in the United States of America
First Edition

CONTENTS

The fire at the Triangle Shirtwaist Factory
(New York Public Library)

one
Fire at the Factory

Across the Hudson River from New York City, in the busy industrial town of Newark, New Jersey, a fire broke out in an old four-story factory building. In just a matter of minutes, the fire spread throughout the old building, and twenty-five factory workers, most of them women, were dead.

The very next day the New York fire chief, Edward Croker, announced "the city might have a fire as deadly as the one in Newark any time. There are buildings in New York where the danger is every bit as great as in the building destroyed in Newark. A fire in the daytime would be accompanied by a terrible loss of life."

No one took heed of Croker's warning. The workers couldn't; they had to go to work or starve. The owners of the factories wouldn't; they needed to stay in business. The landlords of the buildings didn't; they knew that adding more protection for their buildings cost too much money. Nothing changed, and the chief's prophetic words came true.

Exactly four months later, a fire broke out at the Triangle Shirtwaist Factory, in the Asch Building, located in the heart of New York City. Fire fighters tried to rescue workers, but their engine ladders were not tall enough to reach the upper floors in the ten-story building; worse, some workers found themselves trapped, because the fire escape exit doors had been locked.

Out of five hundred employees of the factory—most women, some as young as fifteen, and all immigrants—146 died that afternoon. Trapped and panicking, fifty-four of the girls leapt to their death. The body of a young woman who jumped from the ninth floor got caught on an iron hook outside the sixth floor. It hung there—her clothes still burning—before falling to the sidewalk.

As the fire raged in the Asch Building, thousands of spectators gathered in the streets, unable to tear their eyes from the scene happening so high above them. Two men turned away from the scene, however: Isaac Harris and Max Blanck, the owners of the Triangle Shirtwaist Company. They had narrowly escaped the danger by leaving their tenth floor offices via stairs to the roof and climbing a ladder over to the next building. They were grateful to be alive, and glad that they paid for ample fire insurance. Without it, their business would have been finished. As for the victims of the fire, their employees, Harris and Blanck could do nothing but close their eyes. They certainly were unwilling to take the blame, and a long court battle would ensue to decide once and for all if they were at fault for this workplace tragedy, the worst of its kind in the history of New York City.

Max Blanck (left) and Isaac Harris, owners of the Triangle Shirtwaist
Factory *(Courtesy of UNITE Archives, Kheel Center, Cornell University)*

If it hadn't happened to the Triangle Shirtwaist Factory, a fire of this magnitude would have happened somewhere in the city soon enough. The construction of New York had been so fast, hundreds of skyscrapers existed in New York that were nothing short of firetraps. No one really worried about the threat of fire; between 1901 and 1911, $150,000,000 had been spent in New York to build these skyscrapers. They were the most modern buildings in the world; concrete walls around "skeletons" of steel beams. Because the island of Manhattan was made of bedrock, the foundations for these buildings had been created through the use of dynamite— nothing could make these skyscrapers topple. Nothing like this existed anywhere else in the world, and in New York these buildings were everywhere.

In terms of mileage, New York City is actually quite small—its land area is just 322 square miles. Considering the population, on the other hand, it had become extraordinarily crowded—the largest city in the world. By the early 1900s there was no land left for building new structures. The only way to add on to the city was to rise into the sky. "Limited to the ground, business seeks the air. Confined on all sides, the only way is up," wrote journalist Lincoln Stephens. "When they get crowded they tilt a street on end and call it a skyscraper."

The Triangle Shirtwaist Factory was located in the top three floors of a building named after its prime investor, Joseph J. Asch. The building, constructed in 1901, fit neatly beside the towers containing New York University on the corner of Washington Place and Greene Street, adjacent to Washington Square, a lovely working-class park. Like many buildings of its

New York City in the early 1900s *(Library of Congress)*

kind, the Asch Building was ten stories high, with several of the floors completely open from one end to the other, not compartmentalized into offices. These open floors were called lofts; businesses rented these spaces to be used as factories for manufacturing. With the lofts as open as they were, equipment could be brought in and set up in a way that would maximize the number of workers. In the case of the Triangle Shirtwaist Factory, there were as many as 260 workers crammed on the ninth floor alone. There were approximately 30,000 factories just like this in the city, the majority being on the seventh floor or higher.

At the beginning of the twentieth century there were few laws regarding fire safety in these tall buildings, and the few laws that did exist were not heavily enforced. Asch knew the law required three staircases to be built in his building, because each floor measured about 10,000 square feet. He was a shrewd businessman, however, and didn't want to spend more money than he had to in order to make the building safe. He chose to have only two interior staircases built and got away with it. Buildings were not required at that time to have exterior fire escapes, but Asch had one built to qualify as his third staircase. Only, the fire escape didn't reach all the way to the ground. It actually ended above an enclosed courtyard, at the second floor, hovering over a glass skylight above the basement.

By law, a building more than 150 feet tall had to have metal frames around the windows and stone or concrete floors, but the Asch Building stood at 135 feet, one floor shy of the height required to prevent it from having surfaces made of wood. There were no sprinkler systems, and at that time even the most modern fire engines could not get their ladders and hoses to reach higher than the sixth floor. Any building with factories above seven stories had no real chance in a serious fire.

There were minor fires from time to time in these buildings. None of the previous fires in New York skyscrapers caused great loss of life or property damage, so the general

Different styles of shirtwaists *(Library of Congress)*

public remained unconcerned. A number of fires in factories took place after business hours, which leads to speculation by some historians that they were set on purpose so that companies could get insurance payments.

The employees of the Triangle Shirtwaist Company made women's blouses (shirtwaists). These were a special kind of garment that had very blousy sleeves that tapered down to the wrist where they fit snugly. They were loose around a woman's chest and tight at the waist so as to be tucked into a skirt. In general they were white and crisp, but a shirt-waist could be as simple or ornate as an occasion demanded, which made them suitable for both the working class and Fifth Avenue elite.

These blouses were the most popular item in women's clothing at the beginning of the century thanks mostly to an artist named Charles Dana Gibson. He was an illustrator for fashion magazines and extremely famous for the way he drew modern women. Before photography became inexpensive to reproduce in magazines and newspapers, illustrators did all advertisements and artwork for articles. Gibson was, perhaps, the most famous fashion illustrator of all time. He did most of his work for *Life* magazine, the new periodical that had discovered his talent. His style portrayed modern women as independent, sophisticated, sporty, and energetic. The beautiful women he drew, "Gibson Girls," were both upper-class debutantes and working girls from the city. Susan E. Meyer, author of *America's Best Illustrators* wrote of the Gibson Girl: "She appeared in a stiff shirtwaist, her soft hair piled into a chignon, topped by a big plumed hat. Her flowing skirt was hiked up in back with just a hint of a bustle. She was poised and patrician. Though always well-bred, there often lurked a flash of mischief in her eyes."

Over the years Gibson's artwork became such a sensation that merchandise with his images was sold everywhere and on anything imaginable, including wallpaper. Women from high-class society wanted to model for him, so they could claim to be a Gibson Girl. And today, when one imagines the woman of the Victorian Age in her blousy shirtwaist, slightly bustled ankle-length skirt and tie-up boots twirling a parasol, it is due to Gibson's indelible renderings. From the first published drawing in this fashion, every woman aimed to wear the new shirtwaist style, causing them to be in huge demand.

The problem with this clothing style for the average American woman of the age proved to be the difficulty in making a shirtwaist and in having the time in which to sew one. In the early years of America, all clothing had been

A "Gibson Girl" drawing
by Charles Dana Gibson
(Library of Congress)

handmade. Sewing clothing was an important part of women's education, and many rural women could weave cloth as well. People did not possess more than two or three outfits. In the 1830s general stores began to sell items such as cloaks and capes for women, and pants and jackets for men. These clothing items were generally sized and only needed a minimal amount of tailoring to fit correctly.

During the American Civil War a high demand for soldiers' uniforms created a need to mass-produce items of clothing in ready-to-wear sizes. There simply wasn't enough time or money to provide for fitting each uniform to each man. The revelation that clothes could be made in that manner changed the garment industry forever.

Department stores began to open in major cities, offering the latest fashions for women and men's clothing that required little beyond the addition of some buttons at the waist. Women, who were starting to assert themselves in the workforce, especially enjoyed not having to make their own clothes anymore, freeing up time for other work and joining causes such as the women's suffrage movement. The immigrants and working-class people found that department store clothing was affordable and attractive for them as well.

Department stores needed a huge inventory of ready-to-wear clothes to sell at inexpensive prices. The need for quickly made clothing brought about the rise of the garment factories, and nowhere else in America was the garment-making industry more alive than in New York City.

No one that worked for the Triangle Shirtwaist Company made a whole blouse, no matter how talented a seamstress. Instead, each worker tended to a piece of the product and passed it down the line until it became finished and ready to sell. On the eighth floor of the building resided the designers, cutters, threaders, and some seamstresses. The designers came up with new styles for the blouses; these were usually the best seamstresses. The cutters cut out the pieces that would be sewn together; men always held these positions. The threaders were usually the youngest and most inexperienced workers and their job was to trim the excess thread from a completed garment. Up on the tenth floor resided the offices of the owners, salesmen, and a large room for the pressers who ironed and packaged the clothing. The bulk of the sewing took place on the ninth floor where each woman sat at a sewing machine twelve hours a day sewing the same fraction of a shirt over and over again.

The material used for shirtwaists at Triangle was called lawn, a thin, delicate fabric made of linen or cotton. The sheerness of lawn made it highly flammable. Seamstresses tossed their finished pieces of shirtwaists into a trough between the long tables at which they worked. The scraps went into wicker baskets at their feet. The unfinished pieces remained as such on the tables, ready for work to resume the next time they came in. Cutters kept the scraps from their work in bins below their workspaces. These bins weren't dumped out regularly, because a man named Louis Levy purchased the scraps for his own use. He waited for a large amount of scraps to accumulate before hauling them away. "The last time I removed the rags before the fire was on January 15th, 1911," Levy recalled. "They came from the eighth floor. Altogether, it was, 2,252 pounds." By March 25, more than two months worth of scraps had piled up in each of the cutter's bins.

Nearly all of the employees of the factory were women, many of them young teenagers. All of the employees were immigrants, mostly Italian and Russian. English was a second language for each person, and most barely spoke it at all. They could barely communicate with each other during normal work days. On March 25, 1911, when the fire broke out in the piles of lawn, quickly engulfing the factory, the lack of communication was just one of the many factors that ensured the simple fire would become one of the most infamous tragedies in American labor history.

two
New Yorkers

According to census records, 4,766,883 people lived in New York in 1910. Of that number, roughly 1,944,400 (about 40 percent) were foreign-born. It was the most densely populated city in the world at that time because of an ongoing wave of immigration to the United States primarily from European countries.

In the early 1800s New York had been a fairly rural neighborhood made up of New Englanders that had migrated there after the Revolutionary War. At that time immigrants to the United States arrived through a variety of ports such as Boston, New Orleans, Philadelphia, and Baltimore, in addition to New York, then scattered throughout the expanding country. New York was not the primary drop off place for immigrants who desired to move west of the Atlantic coast because the Appalachian Mountains stood in the way of easy transport.

In 1808 a proposal to connect the Hudson River in the East to Lake Erie in western New York by means of a canal was passed. This canal would be four feet deep, forty feet wide, and rise 568 feet over the mountains. Along the bank of the canal would be a towpath for horses, mules, or oxen to pull boxes along the water. This canal opened up the West to settlers and traders. Upon completion of the Erie Canal in 1825, the main port of entry for immigrants became New York City. Once the immigrants entered the country, they could either choose to stay in New York or travel the canal to start their journey westward. Most chose to stay.

The timing of the Erie Canal's opening, and its subsequent help to the expansion of American land ownership, couldn't

An 1838 engraving of the Erie Canal

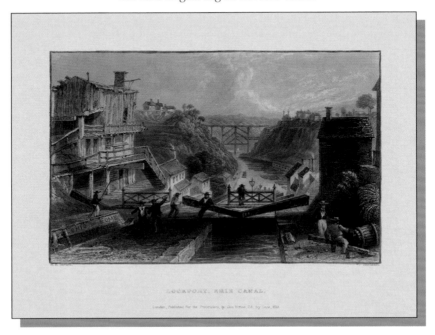

have been better for the people of Ireland. The Irish had been oppressed by the English and were escaping their country in larger numbers each year throughout the early nineteenth century. Between 1845 and 1850 that trickle turned into a flood. A terrible famine set upon the already impoverished country; the one crop the Irish relied upon, potatoes, had failed them. Hundreds of thousands of starving Irish peasants escaped to New York in search of a better life.

The flow of immigrants did not stop there. Another wave began as soon as the Irish began to settle in. This time the immigrants came from the German Confederation. In the nineteenth century Germany was actually a collection of thirty-nine states and free cities. In 1848 a failed revolution against the government sent thousands of Germans into exile. With few choices, most came to the United States. By 1860 one out of every four New Yorkers was German, and by 1875 about 45,000 people in New York were German Jews.

What these ethnic groups had in common was that the American-born residents of New York didn't want them as neighbors. The Irish and Germans got pushed into the same part of town, slums known as the Lower East Side. There they lived in tenements, squalid apartment buildings constructed to the barest minimum of safety regulations and stacked together like dominoes.

The Irish men, having been farmers back home, hired out as laborers, working for the most meager pay, doing heavy jobs such as construction on skyscrapers, digging tunnels for subways, and paving roads with cobblestones. The Germans arrived with more occupational skills and were able to become bankers, shopkeepers, tailors, bakers, shoemakers, and furniture makers. German women, in general,

A 1910 photo of a New York City tenement house *(Library of Congress)*

were usually good at sewing and got jobs as seamstresses. Consequently, the Germans rose more quickly into a life of comfort than the Irish did.

In time, the Irish and German immigrants settled into life in the U.S., finding jobs and prospering, at least enough to leave the Lower East Side. Soon though, they were replaced by a new influx of immigrants, primarily from Italy and Russia.

In the 1880s, Italy suffered agriculturally. The country could not compete with the prices of wheat and citrus North America could afford to charge, and a war between France and Italy had raised the tariffs on wine and other major commodities that supported the country's economics. In a state of severe depression, young Italian men began to leave their villages to find work and send money back home to their families. Often these men went all the way to America, where they would be hired as the cheapest labor available. Usually

A 1900 view of Mulberry Street, located in the center of a predominantly Italian neighborhood in New York City *(Library of Congress)*

the Italians worked temporary jobs then returned to Italy with the money they'd earned. The *prefetto* (government representative) of the province of Cosenza wrote in 1894, "Going to America has become so popular recently that young men feel almost ashamed if they have not been overseas at least once. Ten years ago America evoked images of danger and distance. Now people feel more confident about going to New York than to Rome." Over time, the Italian men would decide to marry in Italy and bring their wives and families back to America with them, finding that the grinding life in New York was still preferable to the desolate life left to them in their home country.

Unlike the Italians, the Russian Jews brought their whole families with them the first time they sailed across the

Atlantic and never intended to return. They were escaping religious persecution that had begun without mercy after the assassination of Czar Alexander II. Unsafe in their homeland, they fled in great numbers to the United States where the Constitution would protect their right to practice their religion freely and safely. These people arrived in America with no money but many old country traditions that were considered strange even to the German Jews already living in the city.

Most of the Russian Jews were skilled laborers, but they could only find work within their own neighborhoods, for every other ethnic group shunned them. "Were we snobby!" said Frances Lehman Loeb, a member of the German-Jewish society. "Only German Jews were even permitted in our circle. For instance, at the Century Country Club . . . there was terrible excitement around our table because they let a Russian Jew in there."

While the Italians and Russians filled up the tenements of the Lower East Side, they did not intermix. Each nationality had its own distinct neighborhoods, entire blocks dedicated to a geographic area or religious belief. Though close in proximity and with similar bigotry facing them from the pre-existing New Yorkers, they did not choose to befriend each other. The only place where they mingled was at work, and that was usually only with the women. Italian men tended to work in building construction or digging subway tunnels. Russian men primarily chose skilled professions within their communities such as shoemaking, carpentry, bookkeeping, or tailoring. The women of both ethnic groups were mostly unskilled and could only find work in low-wage factory work.

By 1910, New York City supplied 70 percent of all the ready-to-wear clothing in the entire country. For that reason, the garment industry had surpassed publishing and printing as the biggest factory industry in the city. However, few clothing manufacturers could afford to make their own clothing, so they looked to find the cheapest workers available to them. These were the most newly arrived immigrants in America, the greenhorns, who needed work and would take any pay offered to them, not knowing better.

These workers, mostly women and girls as young as fourteen, would be gathered up and brought to sweatshops. Sometimes these sweatshops were in loft factories like at the Triangle. However, many times a sweatshop could be twenty women crammed into a one-room tenement apartment with no heat in the winter or cool air in the summer. There might not even be a bathroom in the vicinity. No matter how dismal the location, laborers were forced to work twelve to fifteen-hour days depending upon the business load of the season. During that time they were not allowed to talk to each other, take bathroom breaks, or get up to stretch their legs. They were always crowded together, too many people in too small a space.

Garment workers usually got paid for piecework, meaning that they earned money for each completed piece of the garment they sewed. That could be changed, however. Sometimes, the contractors running the sweatshop would see that a worker was a particularly fast seamstress, so he would no longer pay her for piecework and would give her a weekly salary instead. This way he got away with paying her less than she should have earned. Mistakes or damaged garments got deducted from their pay, and workers often

A group of sweatshop workers in 1908 *(Library of Congress)*

had to supply their own needles and sometimes their own sewing machines.

Many men from the Lower East Side felt that they had paid their dues when they entered the country and now wanted better livelihoods than being grunts. They didn't care if their incomes grew based on the suffering of others. Starting a sweatshop was as easy as finding a location and workers to break their backs for a few pennies a week.

Max Blanck, a Russian immigrant, had been a sweatshop employee until 1895 when he decided to become a contractor. He ran a small business, hiring many relatives and friends to work for him out of his home. His business began to prosper, and then he met Isaac Harris, another Russian, related to Blanck through marriage. Harris had a good business sense about him, or so he claimed. "I laid out the factory and I put in the machines and everything that was done about putting up the factory was done by me," he bragged at one time. The two partnered to open their own business of making shirtwaist blouses just as the fashion was catching on in 1900. They started with a small shop on Wooster Street and called it the Triangle Waist Company. Within two years they were able to move into the new Asch Building on Washington Street and were eventually nicknamed the "Shirtwaist Kings," having the most successful shirtwaist business in the country.

In some ways, when Harris and Blanck moved the Triangle Waist Company into the lofts at the Asch Building, they made some major changes in the way sweatshops were run. Their system was much more organized, and they used electric-powered sewing machines. They had all the most modern equipment, and the building was clean and new. There was even a cloakroom and restroom on each floor. It was definitely a much better working environment than most garment workers had encountered before. It was still considered a sweatshop, though. The working hours were long, the pay low, and the work unending. For all that they had done to advance their business, Blanck and Harris didn't show any real respect or interest in their laborers, only certain that their workers arrived and left as required, and that the output of product was more important than the people who made it.

The only thing that separated factory work from slave labor was that the workers chose to be there and did take home a wage, however meager. While there was a swell of discontent for their situation, many female workers seemed happy to be making a living and were proud of being independent. They had an opportunity to earn an income in

America, which would have been out of the question back home in Italy or Russia. Pauline Cuoio Pepe, a survivor of the Triangle fire related:

> I went to work when I was nineteen. My first job was at the Triangle Shirtwaist Company. I went to work because a woman in the building said to me, "C'mon, we have a lot of fun. What ya doing at home?"
>
> She introduced me to the boss, Mr. Blanck. They hired me as a sewing-machine operator for twelve dollars a week. It was easy work. You just sat there and the machine would run the tucking. I was there almost two years before the fire. We loved it. We used to sing while the machine was going. It was all nice young Jewish girls who were engaged to be married. You should see the diamonds and everything. Those were the ones who threw themselves from the window.

Not all of the workers were so at ease with their situation. That first decade of the twentieth century brought about the rise of workers' unions in New York City, and soon many disgruntled shirtwaist seamstresses would take to the streets in protest of their working conditions.

three
Shirtwaist Workers Strike

The term "sweatshop" doesn't mean to make employees work until they sweat. Rather, it meant that manufacturers sweated out contracts to factory owners to get a certain amount of orders filled within deadlines. It would then be up to the factory owners to turn around and pay contractors (or foremen) to go out and hire immigrants and set up shops in which they could get the work done. As everyone wanted to make the most profit possible, very little money trickled down to the actual people doing the labor.

Louis Hornthal, president of the Clothing Manufacturers' Association, testified in front of a U.S. House of Representatives Committee on Manufacturers in 1892; she denied any knowledge of sweatshop labor. "The committee here from the Clothing Manufacturers' Association are not in a position to give evidence concerning the so-called

Workers in a cramped sweatshop in 1908 *(Library of Congress)*

'sweating system.' We are manufacturers. We give our work out by contract. If any pernicious system exists, we do not know anything about it."

The contractors were immigrants themselves. Sometimes these were cold, hard men who unabashedly used their fellow countrymen and women to work tirelessly for their benefit. At other times, and less often, contractors could be compassionate and simply want to provide a living for friends and family. However, no matter the nature of the contractor's personality or motives, it didn't change the nature of the working conditions. Friendly or harsh, the work was long, tiring, and done in dismal and unsafe surroundings.

At the inception of the sweatshop system in the 1850s all of this kind of work was done in the tenement apartments. These buildings were poorly built, and had few windows for air, light, or circulation. Often the buildings didn't even have bathrooms; one would have to go to an unsanitary outhouse behind the building. Social reformer Jane Addams wrote in 1910, "An unscrupulous contractor regards no basement as too dark, no stable loft too foul, no rear shanty too provisional, no tenement room too small for his workroom as these conditions imply low rental." Sometimes these workshops were in the same places where the contractors lived with their families at night, which meant that it cost the contractor nothing extra in rent for running his business. When the sun came up each day, the workers would arrive, move the beds aside, set up their sewing machines and get to work.

In 1879, the Improved Dwelling Association (IDA) formed with the purpose of bettering the life of the slum areas of New York, particularly in the Lower East Side. One member of the Association, Lawrence Veiller, held fast to his beliefs that life needed to be better for these poor people. He held firm that people had "A God-given right to light and air."

Though for awhile their efforts were thwarted, by 1901 the IDA's efforts forced the enactment of the New Tenement House Law, which ordered windows cut into 350,000 existing tenement apartments along with changes in the way new buildings would be constructed for better sanitation. It was a remarkable triumph even if the small number of building inspectors couldn't get the work completed in any reasonable time frame. The first full inspection of all the buildings constructed before the new law came in effect wasn't until 1908.

When the Triangle Shirtwaist Company opened its new factory in the Asch Building lofts, it did make for slightly better conditions for laborers. At the very least, they weren't crammed into filthy apartments. In fact, Harris and Blanck were particularly proud of their loft space because it provided the 250 cubic feet of air required by law for each employee. It didn't matter to them that the air they referred to was because of ten-foot high ceilings and not due to the distance between workers. They sat packed together, elbow-to-elbow, back-to-back at their tables, barely able to move. The reason behind this tight arrangement of furniture was to maximize the number of sewing machines plugged into one electric motor. The workers put up with the jam-packed conditions because getting to use electric sewing machines was another boon to working for Triangle; many other sweatshops still used foot-pedal machines or even made the workers carry in their own machines from home each day.

While Blanck and Harris outfitted their factory with all the latest equipment, raising the standards and output level in the garment business so that they became the number one company in the market, they still worked their employees hard for little pay. The regard for their employees as people with basic needs was as low as anywhere else in the city. Hours were long, usually twelve a day. When business fell into a slow period, they either fired employees or put them in desperate situations rather than keep them on part time, so at least they could continue making some kind of income. Also, should a worker become ill, she still needed to go to work, for if she missed a day, she could get fired. So, most people trudged into work even if they had high fevers or might collapse at any moment. Like other factories, Triangle workers had few breaks in their day for eating or using the facilities. Triangle workers confessed that they were not allowed to talk while working, and they were penalized for any mistakes that caused goods to be damaged.

Most sweatshop employees kept their complaints silent, afraid to anger their bosses. They needed the work to survive, and many saved what little extra they could to send back to their home countries to family members still stranded in the Old World. Gradually, a few outspoken people began to make a stir.

In 1900 a small group of women organized the Ladies' Waist Makers' Union (LWMU). A union is a group of workers that band together for the purpose of negotiating with company owners for better working conditions. The women in this fledgling union had little support from their peers. If word got out that anyone was involved with this union, they were instantly fired from their jobs. The LWMU was responsible for a handful of small strikes, referred to as wildcat strikes for not being well organized and usually only involving the workers of one business. A strike, or walkout, occurred when business owners refused to concede to any demands from unions for better pay or working conditions. Fed up employees showed up at work in the morning then promptly turned around and walked back out, leaving the factory inoperable and incapable of earning profit. These strikes, if well organized had the power to make changes happen. Small, wildcat strikes were rarely successful, and workers usually wound up going right back to work without a single concession being made for their welfare (if they weren't fired and replaced altogether).

Ultimately the LWMU couldn't stand on its own, and in 1906 the members got absorbed into a much more powerful organization: The International Ladies' Garment Workers' Union (ILGWU). This organization began its operation in England. The men who ran it had little interest in the plight of female workers, believing that women couldn't fight hard enough for rights and were only working temporarily until they got married. Understanding that they were getting little support from the ILGWU as a whole, the seamstresses of New York formed Local 25, a group within the union designed to address the specific needs of the Lower East Side women garment workers. Local 25 was spearheaded by a twenty-year-old woman named Clara Lemlich, a local hero for standing up to authority and surviving horrible beatings from thugs hired to break her resolve. By the end of 1906 they had forty members signed up, one person represented for every 1,000 workers in the industry.

The Local 25 would not have gained much momentum if not for the aid of another group called the Women's Trade Union League (WTUL). Upper-class ladies that didn't need to work in sweatshops but cared about the women who did

Members of Local 25 *(Courtesy of UNITE Archives, Kheel Center, Cornell University)*

made up the bulk of this organization. Women such as these were known as progressives, and they were responsible for providing funds and relief to union workers out on strike.

The WTUL was founded by William English Walling, the son of a Kentucky millionaire who lived in New York and felt strongly about working women in the slums. It disturbed him greatly that so many women had to work for so little pay and that many underprivileged women were forced into prostitution as a way of making ends meet. He created the WTUL in 1903 to "assist in the organization of women wage workers into trade unions."

Soon after its inception he turned the reigns over to influential women like Jane Addams, Lillian

The seal of the National Women's Trade Union League *(Library of Congress)*

Wald, and Eleanor Roosevelt. In 1907 the Dreier sisters took over the WTUL. Margaret Dreier Robins took charge of the Chicago branch of the union, while Mary Dreier became president of the New York League from 1906-1914. This time in history is referred to as the Progressive Era, for being a time instrumental to change in the way industry was run.

By the end of the decade more and more garment workers refused to resign themselves to the degradation of their working environments and strikes became frequent. There were even walkouts at the Triangle Factory. One major walkout happened in 1908, led by a foreman named Jacob Kline who had contracted several of the seamstresses working on the ninth floor. Triangle owners Blanck and Harris believed that hiring several foremen to serve as middlemen between them and the seamstresses would increase competitiveness and relieve them of having to deal personally with any minor employees. Wages for the seamstresses came out of a foreman's paycheck, and he could pay "his" workers whatever he chose. Blanck and Harris failed to realize that many of the foremen cared about the people they hired and genuinely wanted to help them. Kline was one of these good-natured foremen, and on this afternoon he opened his paycheck and found it to be too small to cover what he had promised to pay his contracted workers and still keep enough for himself.

When Kline complained, he was asked to leave the premises. At his continued protest, the company's security guard beat him. Kline pleaded with his co-workers, "Will you stay at your machines and see a fellow worker treated this way?" Every worker rose to their feet, four hundred in all, and walked out of the factory in support of Kline's cause. This walkout proved ineffective and short-lived, as all of the employees, Kline included, returned to work the following week.

Harris and Blanck were terrified of the growing power of the unions. In their opinions, organized labor would mean less profit for them. If seamstresses worked fewer hours and required more pay, they couldn't keep as much money for themselves. They knew that some of their factory workers secretly met with members of Local 25. In September 1909 they sent spies to sit in on a Local 25 meeting and discovered about 150 Triangle employees in attendance. As means of a warning, Harris and Blanck announced that the Triangle Shirtwaist Company would be running its operations through an in-house union called the Triangle Employees Benevolent Association. This was a fake union run by members of the owners' families that represented the best interests of the company. Employees were told that they could work as a member of the in-house union, but if they were caught fraternizing with any other union they would be fired. But instead of frightening the workers into submission, the workers held fast to their resolve. They didn't join the fake union.

The following morning, near the end of September in 1909, the Triangle workers showed up at the Asch Building to find that Harris and Blanck had shut down the factory and locked all of the employees out. If the workers weren't going to follow their rules, they wouldn't get to earn their money. The employees stood on the street and watched as scabs, nonunion workers hired to fill the positions of strikers, were paraded past them and upstairs to do their jobs. Some of the scabs were prostitutes and other people considered of low character. These people were hired specifically as an insult to the regular workers. Fights broke out between those locked out of their jobs and the scabs coming in to fill them, but the union workers didn't give in. They moved from being victims to taking charge of their situation declaring themselves on strike.

They were not alone, either. Within a few days, members from the WTUL joined the strikers. Some of them, mostly well-regarded upper-class women, were even arrested by the police who were all under control of Tammany Hall, the Democratic political force that dominated New York City politics, and in league with the company owners. However,

A group of striking shirtwaist workers, along with some of the prominent women in the community who supported their cause, in 1909 *(Library of Congress)*

when Mary Dreier, the leader of the WTUL joined the cause on November 4, 1909, and got arrested, the strike made headlines for the first time. Her arrest for allegedly threatening to assault a strikebreaker ran on the front page of all the major newspapers, including Joseph Pulitzer's *World* and the *New York Times*.

This shocking news came two days after the city elections that had ripped power completely away from Tammany Hall. The building progressive movement didn't care for the way Tammany Hall favored the business owners and turned police on the strikers and union leaders. The only politician supported by Tammany Hall left in office was the mayor, and he had won only on a slim margin. The public at large was tired of the old ways.

The election, the Triangle strike, the arrests, and the growing violence toward strikers from the police and hired gangsters emboldened garment workers from all over New York. A buzz went through the city amongst the more than 40,000 shirtwaist makers that a general strike of all shirtwaist factories should be declared.

On November 22, 1909, a meeting was held at the Cooper Union's Grand Hall, a brownstone building about four blocks east of the Asch Building. On this night 2,500 workers, both men and women, all employed by shirtwaist factories gathered to listen to speeches by union leaders and prominent figures urging them to band together and fight the injustices put upon them by the factory owners. So many people turned out for this meeting that the crowd spilled over into several other meeting halls in the neighborhood.

For two hours the crowd listened to encouraging pro-union talk, but none of the speakers directly advocated a strike, which is what the workers really wanted from them. In fact, even Samuel Gompers, the head of the American Federation of Labor, one of the most influential union leaders in the country, wavered back and forth on the issue during his speech. At one moment he declared, "There comes a time when not to strike is but to rivet the chains of slavery upon our wrists," while in the next breath he cautioned, "I say, friends, do not enter too hastily." Finally, Clara Lemlich, still recovering from a near-fatal beating by thugs hired to prevent her from aiding a strike against the Leieserson shop in September, stepped out from the crowd. She'd had enough of the waffling and wanted to move this congregation to action.

Samuel Gompers *(Library of Congress)*

"I want to say a few words!" she shouted, interrupting the scheduled program once Gompers finished speaking. The people in the crowd recognized her and enthusiastically helped her to the stage. She didn't have much to say, but what came out had its effect. "I have listened to all the speakers. I have no further patience for talk, as I am one of those who feels and suffers for the things pictured. I move that we go on a general strike."

The listeners rose to their feet cheering and hollering in agreement. It took several minutes to quiet everyone back down. Some of the speakers tried to give gentle warnings that hardship would come with a strike, such as poverty, hunger, and degradation. The words went unheard. At Cooper Union and all the other meeting halls the strike got a unanimous vote. All the shirtwaist workers would walk out of their jobs come Monday morning.

The workers nervously sat at their posts at factories throughout the Lower East Side on the morning of November 23. Some waited up to two hours before finally gathering the courage to stand up and boldly head out the door. Once the movement began, most followed. Outside the buildings, the strikers sought out WTUL and Local 25 leaders to help guide them to meeting halls where they would wait out that first day. The actual picketing began the following morning in two shifts: one in the morning while the strikebreakers showed up to replace them and again in the evenings when it was time for the businesses to close for the day. The intention of striking during that time was to convince the strikebreakers to join them in their cause rather than replace them and make things easier for the owners. The *Call*, a newspaper devoted to the cause of the strikers, declared that 15,000 shirtwaist workers walked out of five hundred shops on that first day. Over the next few weeks that number would swell until the strike became known as the "Uprising of the 20,000."

The union wrote out its demands and had them delivered to the business owners. Chiefly, the workers wanted a shorter workweek of fifty-two hours and a 20 percent pay raise. And the biggest demand of all was that the factories acknowledge the union by hiring only union members, thereby having a closed shop to those who would not join the union. Workplace safety, particularly in the case of fire, is not known to have been discussed.

Most of the shirtwaist shops were less than half the size of the Triangle. Losing their staff made a huge impact on their ability to produce on schedule. They didn't have the nice, relatively clean and safe environment that the Triangle factory offered to the greenhorns that agreed readily to be strikebreakers. Their sweatshops had little about them that was enticing, and, if they wanted to stay in business, they had to give in to the strikers' demands. Seventy of the shops folded to the union within the first two days, capitulating to everything the union asked of them. Those lucky workers were able to return quickly to their jobs and livelihoods.

Panic surged through the owners of the remaining 430 shops. Who would cave next? Who could possibly withstand such a massive strike? The "Shirtwaist Kings," Harris and Blanck, who had already withstood two months of striking by this point, corralled the owners of the top twenty shirt-waist businesses in an emergency meeting to declare that they would not kowtow to the union. They had all of these businessmen sign a document of refusal to recognize a union. By week's end, one hundred other factory owners signed the document as well.

The Triangle owners continued to struggle with their own battle against the strikers; the tactics they used ranging from violent to nurturing. They paid gangsters to rough up union leaders and strikers while at the same time they brought in Victrolas (phonographs) and let the strikebreak-ers dance and sing during their lunch hours. They eagerly sought out any way to divide the strikers or find a weak spot in their stance.

Harris and Blanck noticed quickly that many more of the Jewish employees left their positions to strike than did the Italians. They tried to build on the racial ten-sion between the two groups. One method was to have a Catholic priest come in to the shop and tell the Italians why they would be sinning against the church if they went out on strike. The attempts to divide the workers along these lines failed. Roughly 10 percent of the strikers were Italians, and they didn't suffer any hardship for being the minority group. As the strike went on, various organizations attempted to broaden the racial base of strikers by going up to Harlem and appealing to the primarily African American community that they should not let themselves be hired on as strikebreakers and should side with the union. All races needed better working conditions. Many agreed.

What the Triangle owners missed was the real opposition brewing between the strikers—the motives of those supporting the strikers. The real struggle was between the wealthy progressives (WTUL) versus the poor socialists (Local 25). The progressives believed that all women, rich or poor, were equal to men and should have the right to earn equal pay for equal work. Most of all, however, they stood for women's suffrage. The socialists, on the other hand, were both men and women of the lower classes who had become familiar with the writings of Karl Marx, a Russian philosopher. His work advocated a great disdain for the wealthy and insisted that the government should take over businesses and distribute money and services equally among all people. Socialists were not terribly concerned with the women's right to vote; the bigger concern was to abolish poverty. The two groups had a great deal of difficulty coming to terms with the way the strike should be handled.

Along with the members of the WTUL, several other prominent women stepped up to aide the striking shirtwaist makers. They held parties, parades, and banquets to raise money for the cause. The most outspoken among these well-to-do women were Alva Belmont, a wealthy widow and socialite, and Anne Morgan the daughter of J. Pierpont

Anne Morgan
(above) and Alva
Belmont (right) were
among the members
of the wealthy elite
who championed the
cause of the striking
shirtwaist workers.
(Library of Congress)

Morgan, a titan in the steel industry. Because of their influence, the strike repeatedly made headlines in all the biggest newspapers. More shirtwaist companies folded under the pressure of the publicity.

The Socialists from the Lower East Side were not appreciative of the efforts from Belmont, Morgan, and their friends. While they couldn't deny that the extra financial support to the cause provided from the WTUL's events was a good thing and allowed the strike to continue for so many weeks, they feared the point of the strike was being lost in rhetoric about women's votes. The differences in point of view caused a lot of aggravation for the strikers who didn't know which leaders to follow.

When the strikers felt at their strongest, in December of 1909, they had declined the Triangle's offer to accept the terms of shorter hours and better pay—but no closed union shop. Two months later, on February 8, 1910, when the Triangle owners offered the same deal, the tired, hungry, and confused workers accepted and went back to work.

For the next year they dutifully attended their sewing machines, happy to have achieved a victory, yet anxious to begin talks about the other workplace concerns that had gone ignored in the strike. For example, when would the Union begin to negotiate for a safer working environment? Unfortunately, 146 of them had to die before talks began again.

four
Fire from the Outside

As the seasons passed the general public forgot the plight of the shirtwaist workers. It was the beginning of spring in 1911, more than a year since the strike ended. The weather was clear and warm with a slight breeze. It was a Saturday, and those who didn't have to work were enjoying a day out at the Washington Square Park or shopping in the city.

Thousands of New Yorkers passed the Triangle Shirtwaist Factory every day, because it was located at a busy intersection of the city, just around the corner from the park. None of them wondered what might be happening to the workers high above them, past the Triangle sign hanging from the corner of the building. But that afternoon several people in the vicinity heard a loud puff and the breaking of glass. Within minutes the streets around the Asch Building were packed with people craning their necks to the spectacle of desperate Triangle employees crammed in the building's windows struggling to figure out how to survive the fire consuming the lofts behind them.

At 4:45 p.m., a laborer named Dominick Cardiane was pushing a wheelbarrow past the Greene Street entrance to the building. Suddenly, the windows far above him exploded and rained down broken glass on his head. A horse tied to a wagon in the street whinnied and ran off. John H. Mooney, a businessman, stepping out from his workplace, saw Cardiane and looked up at the source of the shattered glass and saw smoke billowing out of the windows on the eighth floor. He immediately rushed to the nearest fire alarm box and pulled it.

On the other side of the building, newspaper reporter William Gunn Shepherd ran from Washington Square at the sight of smoke coming from the eighth floor windows of the building, but he was passed by a mounted policeman named James Meehan who was galloping at full speed toward the Washington Place entrance. Shepherd stayed outside to watch the events unfold and would, in the end, write a detailed and dramatic article about the spectacle for the United Press news agency. The article would become the most important piece in his career. Meehan jumped off his horse in the middle of the street and went inside to help.

The Asch building sat on the corner of Washington Place and Greene Street. The main entrance was midway along the Washington Place side, and midway along the Greene Street side of the building was the service entrance. The lobby of the building was square and open. A person stepping inside could see straight across to the other entrance. There were many windows to the outside, and the two walls of the building that did not face the street were either attached to the adjoining buildings or had windows opening to an enclosed courtyard. By the Greene Street entrance were two freight elevators side-by-side and a narrow stairwell. Two smaller passenger elevators were near the Washington Place entrance and stairwell.

Meehan saw right away that the freight elevators were at the top floors when he entered the building, so he bounded up the Washington Place stairs. Around the fifth floor Officer Meehan met up with the first wave of girls winding their way down the narrow staircase to safety. He let them squeeze past and continued upward. Closer to the seventh floor he helped revive a woman that had fainted, blocking the escape route for everyone else. Her name was Eva Harris, Isaac Harris's sister.

When Meehan finally reached the eighth floor, the heat from the fire was unbearable. With the help of a Triangle machinist named Louis Brown, he managed to help two girls who were poised to hurl themselves out the windows. The men pulled them back and got them down the stairs just before the smoke made it impossible for them to stay any longer.

Only five minutes after having left his horse, Meehan reemerged from the building. In that short time the scene outside had changed dramatically. The fire fighters had begun to arrive in their horse-drawn wagons, seven in all, plus a couple of the first motorized fire units. With their clanging bells and shrill whistles, they made their presence known.

The noise and commotion brought more people running to the scene to see what was going on. A huge crowd began to amass around the building. Frank Fingerman, who worked in another building on Washington Place said, "The crowds

A horse-drawn fire engine on its way to the Triangle Factory fire
(Library of Congress)

were jamming our own door until I could not pass out and the street was packed right up to the fire trucks." Worse than that, however, was that the fire had become out of control up above them, and the trapped workers had already begun to seek their only way out—jumping from the windows.

The first woman jumped only a moment after Officer Meehan had run inside the building. He missed it, but bystander James Cooper did not. Right after that first explosion of the windows, he saw what he thought was "a bale of dark dress goods" come out of a window above him. Someone standing near him agreed dimly that it was probably someone from the factory trying to save the best material in the shop from burning. That was not the case.

Charles Willis Thompson wrote to a colleague about his moment of understanding:

> It looked like a parcel of some kind of goods, reduced to ashes. It had no shape, and was just a parcel of cinders. I looked at it for some time, idly wondering why they should have dumped that package of burned goods on the sidewalk. Then I saw the top of it, with congealed blood on it. The top was a neck. Head, arms, and legs were all gone, which accounted for its peculiar shape.

The screaming of falling women caught the attention of Lena Goldman, who owned a restaurant up the street at which many of the Triangle employees frequented. "The screams brought me running," she said. "I could see them falling! I could see them falling!"

Martha Dolinko, an underage worker at a factory across the street from the Asch building remembered, "My God, the people couldn't get out. The windows were shut, so some of them with their feet broke the windows and they jumped. Oh, I'll never forget. I close my eyes and zip goes a girl."

Some tried to help. The *New York Times* recorded a story told by Benjamin Levy, a junior executive of a whole clothing manufacturer a couple blocks away:

> I was upstairs in our work-room when one of the employees who happened to be looking out of the window cried that there was a fire around the corner. I rushed downstairs, and when I reached the sidewalk the girls were already jumping from the windows. None of them moved after they struck the sidewalk. Several men ran up with a net which they got somewhere, and I seized one side of it to help them hold it.
>
> It was about ten feet square and we managed to catch about fifteen girls. I don't believe we saved over one or two however.

The fall was so great that they bounced to the sidewalk after striking the net. Bodies were falling all around us, and two or three of the men with me were knocked down. The girls just leaped wildly out of the windows and turned over and over before reaching the sidewalk.

The Asch Building happened to be in the vicinity of one the city's first high-water-pressure hydrants. This was the most modern way of fighting fires devised. To get the most pressure possible to a hydrant, engineers at the nearest pumping

Fire fighters work to extinguish the fire in the Asch Building. *(Courtesy of Keystone/Getty Images)*

station turned shut-off valves to send all the water toward a particular hydrant. However, while trying to dodge the falling bodies and keep the horses from bolting out of fear, the first two teams of fire fighters to reach the scene struggled to get the hoses hooked up to the water supply. "We had to lift them off before we could get to work," Fire Captain Howard Ruch explained.

Ruch led his crew up the Greene Street stairwell moments after a team led by fire fighter Oliver Mahoney headed up the Washington Place stairwell. By the time the fire fighters reached the eighth floor, the loft was completely engulfed in flames. They aimed their hoses into the room and worked at extinguishing the fire. The heat was so intense and the smoke so thick that the two teams could not see each other from across the room.

On the street other crews of fire fighters hurried to get out their life nets to break the fall of the jumpers, but they knew it would be a pointless effort. Fire Chief Edward F. Croker testified in court later that he knew "It would be impossible to hold those people as they fell there; when they hit the sidewalk or iron gratings, the impact of their bodies was so great they drove right through the iron gratings into the cellar." He explained further that he knew the nets could hold someone jumping from six stories high, but "Seven or eight stories high, if they jump, I don't know of anything you can manufacture that will hold them. I saw it figured out for a body weighing 150 pounds, they struck over two tons from that height when they hit the sidewalk."

Unfortunately he was right; the nets didn't hold. The girls broke straight through them. Battalion Chief Edward J. Worth agreed. "What good were life nets? The little ones went through

Observers stand around a hole in the sidewalk caused by a falling factory worker. *(Courtesy of New York Public Library)*

life nets, pavement, and all. I thought they would come down one at a time. I didn't know they would come down with arms entwined — three and even four together."

An ambulance wagon from St. Vincent's hospital pulled into the scene, and the driver tried to position his vehicle so that it might stop the fall of some jumpers too. The bodies just bounced off the roof and splattered on the ground beside it.

Screams from the crowd begged the desperate workers in the ninth floor windows not to jump. They knew now that the nets wouldn't catch anyone, but the bodies continued to come down. The firefighters tried to raise their ladders high enough to help extinguish the fire or catch some of the jumpers, but they simply could not reach any higher than the seventh floor and proved useless. One woman jumped from the ninth floor aiming for a ladder and missed by a large margin.

Her arms flailed as she plummeted towards the ground, the ladder far from her grasp.

But this was only on the Washington Place side of the building. These jumpers took their time, decided on suicide and leapt. On the Greene Street side, the situation was much more severe. Reporter Shepherd responded to a giant rise in the amount of screaming on the Greene Street side of the building and got around the corner just in time to see a slew of workers who had been backed up against the windows by the flames fall out in one giant, burning, wailing heap. It was a sight that he would never be able to shake off.

While Shepherd's tale rings of authenticity—the truth of a man who saw for himself the events as they played out—other newspaper accounts tended to sensationalize. There were many tales bandied about regarding miraculous recoveries or horrific deaths. One story told of a woman who fell into a life net and crawled out alive; she supposedly walked ten steps before collapsing to the ground and dying. Another grand but morbid article told of a group that tried to escape from the building by forming a human chain from the ninth floor window to the window of a building across the courtyard. Supposedly, the first few women were able to cross safely, but the weight of those crossing broke the back of the man linked in the middle and the people still trying to cross all fell to their deaths. These stories are quite impossible, of course. No one could have lived through the fall to stand and walk, and no reporter could have seen a human chain ladder from one building to the other, as there was no access to the courtyard between the adjoining buildings from the street.

All efforts to assist the Triangle workers did not end in vain, however. Next door at New York University, a law professor named Frank Sommer had been teaching a class of fifty students in a tenth-floor classroom when he heard the fire engine sirens. After glancing out the window to see what was happening, he burst into action. He called for his students to follow him to the roof, whereupon they used two ladders to form a bridge from the top of the Asch Building to the university building. All but one of the tenth-floor employees' lives were saved by climbing across to the neighboring buildings. The only person to die from the tenth floor had jumped from a window in panic.

Another hero that evening was Thomas Gregory. He ran the elevator at 103 Bleecker Street and was passing by

Most of the tenth-floor workers were able to escape the fire by climbing to the roof of the Asch Building, and crossing a ladder to the rooftop of a New York University building. *(Courtesy of FPG/Getty Images)*

the Asch Building, headed home, when the fire broke out. According to the *New York Times* account, he went into the building and found one elevator at the upper floors while the other one remained on the ground floor without an operator. He jumped in and took the elevator up for three trips to rescue fire victims. Apparently the desperate workers were so frantic to get into the elevator and down to safety that they clawed and pushed at each other to the point that he even got nails dug into his neck and face. Regardless of the pain, he saved lives until he could no longer dare to take the elevator up again.

The heat of the fire had blown out the windows of the New York University law library across the airshaft from the ninth floor of the Asch Building. Students and faculty members scrambled to save their valuable book collection from being destroyed.

The fire only lasted about half an hour, but the vision of it would remain in the minds of the people out on the street forever. As William Shepherd wrote at the closing of his famous article:

> The floods of water from the firemen's hose that ran into the gutter were actually stained red with blood. I looked upon the heap of dead bodies and I remembered these girls were the shirtwaist makers. I remembered their great strike of last year in which these same girls had demanded more sanitary conditions and more safety precautions in the shops. These dead bodies were the answer.

five
The Fire Inside

It happened fast—thirty-five minutes from start to finish. The four-thirty bell rang. Some workers jumped up from their seats to grab their coats and head out the door as fast as they could. They had Saturday night plans. Others took their time, finally having the opportunity after a long day to talk with their friends. They all left their unfinished work on the tables next to the sewing machines or in wicker baskets beside their chairs. None of them gave the bundles of cloth a second thought. All they wanted was to be done with their long workweek and get out of the building for some rest and well-deserved relaxation.

About five minutes earlier, someone broke the rules and lit a cigarette. It might have been Isadore Abramowitz, for the cigarette got tossed into his trash bin, a wooden container full of scraps of material from the cutting table where he worked. It might have been someone else, for Abramowitz admitted to seeing the flames rise up from his trash bin. He did not confess to smoking the cigarette butt that fire marshals later claimed to have caused the whole blaze.

When Joseph Wexler, the eighth-floor watchman rang the quitting bell, the cigarette butt in Isidore Abramowitz's scrap bin had already started a blaze that had begun to take over the whole side of the room.

About 180 people worked on the eighth floor of the Triangle Shirtwaist Factory. Most of the men of the company worked on this floor as cutters. They had the difficult and demanding job of cutting out the patterns for the blouses out of the lawn material. It took a great deal of strength and precision for them to use the special knives and slice through many layers of cloth to create as many pieces at one time as possible. They also had to plan their work so that they used as much of the material as possible—wasted material meant less profit. The finished pieces got distributed to the seamstresses and the excess material got dumped into the large bins under the table. They sat at seven long rows of wooden tables parallel to Greene Street.

The rest of the open room was filled with sewing tables twice as long as the cutting tables and filled with electric sewing machines all connected to one power source. Nearly every table in the large loft ran parallel except for two shorter tables in the back of the room going the opposite direction and subsequently blocking the path to the fire escape. There were no walls on the eighth floor, save for a partition for the dressing rooms and restrooms on the west side.

Abramowitz's bin was one table away from the Greene Street stairs and freight elevator. No sooner did the fire alight but a draft from the airshaft near the elevator caught it and

The fire started in this area of the factory. *(Courtesy of New York Public Library)*

began blowing it up to the ninth and tenth floors. Up on the ninth floor Anna Gullo rang the quitting bell at 4:45, completely unaware that a fire had begun just below her and that smoke was just beginning to eke into the room.

On the eighth floor the fire fighting had already begun. A seamstress named Eva Harris reported smelling smoke to Samuel Bernstein, the Triangle's production manager, who happened to be sitting with Dinah Lipschitz at her distribution desk. Bernstein immediately rushed to Abramowitz's table and joined several cutters trying to douse the flames with water buckets. This proved useless. Instead of dousing the fire, every pail of water caused the fire to grow wilder—the lawn material was highly flammable, and the water served to just spread around the oil and grease that was fueling the fire.

Bernstein thought he was helping when he joined in the bucket brigade, but his efforts made no difference. The fire continued to grow. And it was only made worse when the man operating the Greene Street elevator, who had been sitting waiting for workers to start heading downstairs for the day, ran out to help with the water buckets. When he did this, he left his elevator doors open, and the draft that ran from the street up the elevator shaft stoked the flames.

Bernstein persisted with the pails anyway, mindless of the fact that the water was not helping. Then a man named Louis Senderman entered the loft from the Greene Street stairwell. He had run down from the tenth floor. Together, he and Bernstein retrieved the fire hose in the stairwell and turned the knobs that should have brought water down from the reserve on the roof of the building. The hose didn't work; there wasn't enough pressure. Bernstein climbed up onto a table and finally realized, "The fire was running away from me." He had wasted too much time saving the building and now needed to focus on saving the workers.

People ran in every direction, desperate for an escape. Some went to the Greene Street stairwell. Many more headed for the Washington Place stairwell, because it was farther away from the blaze. But the Washington Place exit was a dead-end—the door was locked. At quitting time on a regular day, Joseph Wexler opened the Greene Street door where he would stand and check every woman's pocketbook for stolen goods, then the employees would be released one at a time down those stairs—no one ever left through the Washington Place stairs. However, panicked workers plowed toward it, smashing the people closest to the door into it, suffocating them.

Some quick thinkers climbed over the tables and busted out the windows to get to the fire escape. A few got on the Washington Place elevators, which stopped only once to pick up passengers on that floor.

From his vantage point on top of the table, Bernstein was amazed to see many workers in the frenzy were still bothering to go to the dressing room to collect their coats and pocketbooks. They weren't heading for the exits. He also saw the people jammed up at the locked Washington Place stairwell door.

He tried to take control of the situation. First, he grabbed Louis Brown, the sewing plant machinist, and pointed to the Washington Place door. "Try to get the girls out as quick as you can!" he ordered Brown. Then he jumped down from the tables and started pushing the rest of the workers toward the Greene Street exit. "I just drove them out," he explained later.

Brown encountered some difficulty getting the Washington Place stairwell door open. It was designed to open into the room, but so many bodies were pressing up against it, that he had to pull people back out of the way to be able to reach it, unlock it, and pull it open. "I had to push the girls away from the door," he explained. "I couldn't open it otherwise. They were packed there by the door, you couldn't get them any tighter. I pulled with all my strength. . . . But they were all against the door and while I was pulling to open it they were pushing against it as they tried to get out." By the time he managed to do this, he saved Ida Cohen, a sewing machine operator, from being crushed to death by the throng.

Through all of Bernstein's and Brown's heroics, Dinah Lipschitz had been doing her best to let the other floors

The inward-opening doors that prevented easy access to the stairwell
(Courtesy of New York Public Library)

know about the fire emergency. She had tried sending a message, "FIRE!" to the tenth floor on a machine called the TelAutograph, an early version of the fax machine. This machine was designed so that she could write a message, and the receiving device on the tenth floor would scrawl it out simultaneously. However, it rarely worked, and on this day it failed. Up on floor ten, Mary Alter, who happened to be filling in at the front desk that day for the regular reception-ist, heard the buzz that signaled a message was coming, but the message never came. Lipschitz waited two minutes, an incredible amount of time given the chaos happening around her, before she realized the message hadn't gotten through. Finally, she picked up the phone and called.

Alter panicked at the screaming coming from eighth-floor phone line. Instead of hanging up and clearing the line, she dropped the receiver and ran off to find her bosses, Blanck and Harris. As the phone dangled uselessly off Alter's desk, Lipschitz sat frustrated and desperate two floors down—she could not call the ninth floor and alert them. She screamed at Bernstein, "I can't get anyone! I can't get anyone!"

Bernstein knew that he had to go up there himself and warn everyone. The eighth floor was now empty, so he told Dinah Lipschitz to head downstairs to safety, and he set off for the ninth floor. It was now 4:48 p.m.

Outside, the witnesses had begun to gather. The first few calls to the fire stations had been made, and the first fire truck was pulling up outside. Some eighth-floor survivors had made it to the ground floor while Officer Meehan and fire fighters met others on the stairs. In the Washington Place stairwell Meehan and Brown heard banging against the locked door to the sixth floor loft. They busted the door open to find

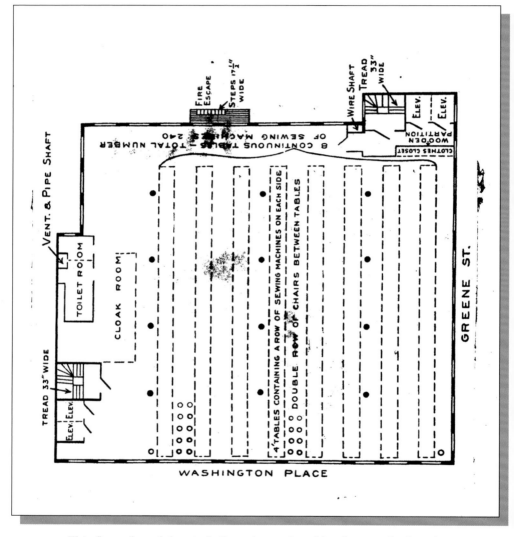

This floor plan of the ninth floor shows the tables that ran the length of the room, and the Greene and Washington Street stairwells.

(Courtesy of UNITE Archives, Kheel Center, Cornell University)

several eighth-floor workers that had climbed in through the windows from the fire escape. These lucky survivors had realized that the fire escape could not get them all the way to solid ground. It ended above glass skylights to the basement in an L-shaped courtyard between the three buildings with no access to the street. So, as soon as they were safely below the fire, they searched for a way back inside the building. They had not expected to get trapped in the room. Now they took the stairs down to the lobby.

Up on the ninth floor, the fire had finally taken hold and began blazing across the room. Many workers rushed to the fire escape. Workers on the tenth floor headed for the fire escape as well. The thin, metal structure was not built for the amount of weight being put upon it, and it buckled under the sudden influx of weight. People quickly realized they had to get off the fire escape fast, but the metal shutters that allowed

The buckled metal shutters that blocked the traffic flow on the fire escape *(Courtesy of New York Public Library)*

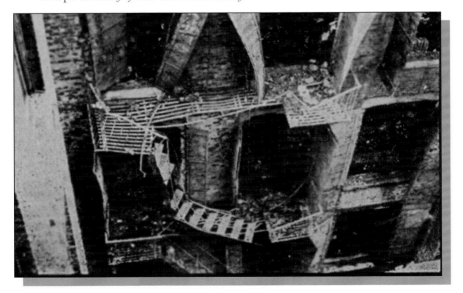

access to the fire escape from the windows opened outward, blocking the traffic flow every time they were opened. One of these shutters got stuck in its open position at the seventh floor, and another stuck at the tenth floor. The workers couldn't get them to budge. More and more people pushed onto the steps, but no one could move. The fire licked at their clothes and set them ablaze.

Then, with a clanging screech and moan, the fire escape pulled away from the building and collapsed. All of the workers on the fire escape were thrown to their deaths, falling hundreds of feet to the ground below.

Inside, an elevator operator named Joseph Zito, and several others, took groups of passengers from the eighth floor, one load at a time, then went back up to make two stops on the tenth floor and another three stops on the ninth. When the elevators arrived on the tenth floor, word had only just arrived about the fire and some smoke was billowing up from the airshaft.

The tenth-floor employees were primarily the executives, salespeople, designers, and pressers. Harris and Blanck had offices, but most of the room was open for the pressers to do their work. Zito opened his elevator door to find a group of frenzied people who didn't know in which direction to go. He saw Blanck standing on top of a table with two of his daughters; they had come to work with their nursemaid that afternoon to accompany him shopping after work. Blanck was frightened and seemed paralyzed with indecision. However, when his young daughter went to run into the elevator, he grabbed her arm and pulled her back out again. The elevator went down and didn't come back to that floor again.

The flimsy fire escape collapsed after the workers crowded onto it.
(Courtesy of New York Public Library)

Joseph Zito, the elevator operator who made several trips to the burning floors to bring workers down to safety *(Courtesy of UNITE Archives, Kheel Center, Cornell University)*

Things on the ninth floor were much worse when Zito finally brought his car to a stop there. The entire floor was on fire, and the workers were pressing themselves against the elevator doors. "When I first opened the elevator door on the ninth floor all I could see was a crowd of girls and men with great flames and smoke right behind them," he said later. They squeezed themselves so tightly into the elevators that they could barely breathe. Not an inch was left unoccupied. Two more times Zito managed to bring the elevator up again, but on the last trip he knew the fire was burning too hot for him to try again. "When I came to the floor the [last] time, the girls were standing on the window sills with the fire all around them," he recalled.

Sensing the elevators weren't coming back up, the women became frantic. The smoke made it impossible to see or breathe. They ran wildly, unable to think clearly. Few spoke English; they screamed and shouted in their native tongues, unable to understand each other. Lena Yaller, a ninth-floor worker, recalled, "I could not make out what they did say, simply. It was so many languages. . . . They all spoke in another language. The smoke and all. And some were screaming about their children." Without the ability to communicate clearly with each other to make a plan, people began acting without thinking. They did anything they thought might help them survive—or at least keep them from burning.

A seventeen-year-old girl named Katie Weiner testified that she swung herself into an elevator as it descended. The door was still open enough for her to slide down the cable into it. She landed on the heads of all the passengers and rode down upside down, her feet in the air banging against the sides of the elevator shaft. Others grabbed onto cables after the elevator stopped and tried to slide all the way down to the roofs of the elevators. But the skin of their hands and legs burned off from the friction, and they tumbled down with nothing to slow their fall. Those who didn't die in the plunge or get smothered by bodies falling in on top of them were severely wounded and scarred. Some even desperately flung themselves into the elevator shaft with their clothes and bodies on fire, plummeting to their deaths. The bodies piled up on top of the elevators.

"A body struck the top of the elevator and bent the iron," Zito said. "I knew the poor girls up there were trapped. But my car wouldn't work. It was jammed by the bodies."

It was now about 4:50 in the afternoon, just ten minutes after the fire had started. The ninth-floor workers had already discovered that the Washington Place stairwell door

The top of the elevator was crushed by the falling bodies of panicked workers who jumped down the elevator shaft to escape the fire. *(Courtesy of New York Public Library)*

was locked. The Greene Street stairwell was now filled with fire and impassable. The fire escape had collapsed, and the elevators were no longer running. There was nowhere left to go but out the windows.

The workers ran to the windows, already shattered from the heat of the fire. A man jumped; he was the first.

On the Washington Place side, they went with almost a sense of calm and resignation. They made the choice to jump and went bravely. Some held hands. One man carefully aided several women by holding them out over the ledge and dropping them before following them. Some surely knew that they would die.

On the Greene Street side, things were not as calm. The fire was at its worst on that side of the building. The women on that side were trapped closer to the flames, and their clothes and hair had caught on fire. Flames pushed at them until they had no choice at all.

At about 4:57, in a great heap, about forty women, their clothes and hair in flames, tumbled out the windows together. One woman's dress caught on the Triangle sign outside the building. She hung there, safe for a second, then the fire burned through the fabric, and she tumbled down to the street below.

Somewhere between eighty and ninety workers were still trapped and would not make it out at all.

Meanwhile, on the tenth floor, Harris led everyone to the Greene Street stairwell, leading to the roof. This was not an easy route, by any means. The fire outside in the airshaft had grown so powerful it had blasted the windows all along the Greene Street side of the building. To get to the stairs they had to go right through the flames. People wrapped their faces with lawn material or grabbed coats and muffs to shield their skin. These wrappings burned but saved many employees from serious injury. Still, clothing and hair caught on fire, and as soon as they got out of the stairwell, many had to roll around on the rooftop to get the flames out.

Bernstein managed to make it up to the tenth floor, bypassing the ninth where he could be of no help, and helped with Harris's evacuation. Bernstein had to haul Louis Silk down from a table where he stubbornly tried to break a skylight above him, and he slapped Lucy Wesselofsky back to consciousness after she fainted in the middle of the flaming room.

Harris calmly led his staff to climb up above the elevator shaft roof and across to the adjoining building rooftops that were a floor higher than the Asch Building. There was no way to climb up, and for a moment the tenth-floor employees thought they were stranded. But with a strength that surprised him and those following him, Harris leaped as high as possible to scale the wall of the neighboring building, the American Book Building. He got hold and climbed over the top. Once up there, he reached over the side and helped others climb up. Those on the Asch building roof helped boost from below.

On the far side of the roof, more tenth-floor employees were being aided by the NYU law students by crossing over on ladders. One 250-pound man had to be cajoled up the ladder. A woman who had fainted had to be dragged across by her hair.

Bernstein got to the roof last and there was no one left to boost him up to the American Book Building. The fire was growing more intense in the airshaft, burning through the

A view of the factory after the fire *(Courtesy of New York Public Library)*

skylights. He ran to the ladders leading to the NYU building and crossed to safety at approximately 5:00 p.m.

Fifteen minutes later, the fire was extinguished.

six

Claiming the Dead

While the fire was under control by 5:15 Saturday
evening, the heat continued to be intense for the
fire fighters up on the top three floors of the Asch
Building. And they now had to deal with the dead bodies
scattered outside on the ground and inside the building. The
bodies needed to be recovered and sent somewhere for iden-
tification. Meanwhile, the crowd on the street continued to
multiply into the thousands, people from all corners of the
city coming to find people they knew or just to gawk. The job
ahead for the fire fighters, police, and medical workers was
intense, and it took three crew shifts and well into Sunday
morning for them to get through it all.

The first major problem was keeping the crowd at bay.
Once the last body fell, the onlookers couldn't control the
urge to break forward and get to the victims on the ground.
Desperate parents and family members needed to know

A crowd of onlookers at the scene of the fire *(Library of Congress)*

if their daughters or sisters were amongst those who had fallen. Even though ropes had been strung to keep the people back, the crowd pushed through, knocking them down. Some grabbed up belongings that had fallen to the street like purses, shoes, and hats.

The police had to use their clubs a few times to keep the crowd back and under control. It was strangely reminiscent of the time only a little more than a year before when these very same officers raised their clubs against the Triangle workers out on strike. These men that were once arresting sixteen-year-old girls and sending them to jail or workhouses for speaking out against unfair treatment were now protecting their dead, broken bodies.

Once the throng was effectively held at bay, authorities laid out a red tarp on Greene Street and began to lay about forty of the corpses in rows upon it in a more orderly fashion. The police covered the bodies as best they could with tarpaulins. Then they gathered up all the debris that had fallen with them such as pocketbooks, watches, shoes, hats, and money. All of these belongings were sent to the Mercer Street station house to be sorted.

The Triangle employees who had been held inside the lobby until the rain of bodies stopped were also eager to find their friends and relatives among the dead outside. Some were simply dazed and wandered about outside not sure of where to go or what to do next. Others groped about the fallen bodies until policemen guided them across the street, away from the ghastly scene. "I had a lot of friends who were killed," said Pauline Cuoio Pepe. "Then I had one friend—when we got down, I was looking for her. Sure enough, she was there. She was looking for me. Oh, my God, we hugged each other, and this man saw us crying. He said, 'Oh, don't worry, we'll take you home.' We told him where we lived, and they were very nice to take us home."

Some survivors like Pepe and Ethel Monick made it home so bloody and disheveled that family members who had not heard news of the fire thought they had been raped or mugged. Others like Dora Appel and Rose Cohen managed to get back to their homes to find them empty; their roommates and relatives had gone to search for them. They woke from exhausted sleep to the relieved screams of loved ones returning to find them alive after a long night of looking at charred dead bodies. And finally there were those who made it home but had left brothers, sisters, or parents behind at work and waited, hoping upon hope that their relatives would follow soon. A few, like Isadore Wegodner, were lucky. He found his bedraggled father at the train station. "I remember how with my last strength I shouted to him, how I went tearing over the little bridge that connected the two platforms, how we fell into each other's arms and how the people stopped to look while sobbing he embraced me and kissed me."

The overwhelming majority of survivors did not leave the area. Some waited to find out the fate of their coworkers and friends, and others were too badly burned or injured to leave the scene on their own. Ambulances arrived, and medics did their best to wrap burns and splint broken bones before helping the frazzled Triangle workers into the wagons.

At six o'clock the heat inside the building had finally cooled enough to allow a new team of firefighters to get inside and begin looking for survivors. Amazingly, there were a handful of people still alive. Sarah Cammerstein was found unconscious in the elevator shaft under nineteen dead and dying bodies. Hyman Meshel had somehow jumped in the elevator shaft underneath the elevator and was in the very pit of the shaft barely hanging on to life. All the water that had been used to put out the fire was pooling up around him, and he would have soon drowned if not for keen firefighters who heard his weak cries. Maurice Samuelson didn't work for the Triangle Shirtwaist Company. He ran his own business, Samuelson and Company, on the second floor of the Asch building. He had been in his office when he heard the sirens. The sight of the burning bodies flailing past his windows paralyzed him with fright. Fire fighters had to help him out of the building.

Coffins arrived on the scene at about 7:00 p.m. The police had ordered about one hundred coffins from the city morgue, but they only came up with sixty-five. They quickly realized that this number was not going to be nearly enough as the fire fighters inside the building started sending more corpses down by way of block-and-tackle hoists attached to the roof of the building. One by one they lowered bodies found in the lofts, a searchlight spotlighting the journey of each one to the ground. Fifty-four bodies had been counted as having jumped or fallen from the windows, about twenty-four had fallen from the broken fire escape, and over the next few hours close to sixty bodies were lowered from above.

At this point the rescuers hadn't even realized there were more fatalities in the elevator shafts and fallen through the skylights of the basement. It had become clear, though, that not only were they going to be short of coffins but the city morgue would not have enough room for so many bodies.

Bodies of factory workers being placed in coffins *(Library of Congress)*

The shipment of coffins were filled and sent to the morgue while another team of workers went to the pier to build a makeshift morgue near the water.

The city officials took over the Charities Pier, where Twenty-Sixth Street ended at the East River, and converted it into a temporary resting place for the deceased until they could be identified and removed. The pier had an iron-frame structure covering it to provide some protection from the elements. The pier became known as Misery Lane.

The crowd split for a while once the news got out that some belongings had been sent to the Mercer Street station house three blocks away. Many took turns going there, searching for any sign of lost friends and loved ones. They dug through

Fire fighters search for bodies. *(Library of Congress)*

the trays of items, looking for something familiar, but few found what they needed for comfort. When they were done at the station house, they'd head over to the city morgue or St. Vincent's Hospital. Back and forth again they went through the night. Most of these trips were made in vain, but it kept at least a few hundred people occupied during the early hours after the fire. In the end, most returned to the crowd outside the Asch Building, where two lines were forming, heading toward Misery Lane.

At ten-thirty more coffins arrived, supplied by the Metropolitan Hospital's carpentry shop. They were brought to the scene by twenty-five derelicts forced to volunteer from the Municipal Lodging House on East Twenty-Fifth Street. The remaining bodies were loaded into the coffins, and sturdy wagons toted three to four at a time down to the pier, clanging bells as they went both to call attention to the dead and to clear the way for passage.

Forty-five minutes later, the last body was lowered from the ninth floor. At 11:30 Fire Chief Croker told the press, "My men and I have gone through every floor, every room in the building. We have gone through the basement, we have gone through the airshaft at the rear of the building. Every body has been removed."

Inspector Richard Walsh had taken charge of the organization of Misery Lane. He had each coffin numbered, and that number corresponded with a description of the body and any belongings still on the person that he recorded in a notebook. To the best of their ability, the police kept the bodies the way they were received, and that meant they were often still wearing their jewelry and shoes. In one case a woman had a large sum of money stuffed into her stocking. Because so many of the bodies were burned beyond recognition, it was hoped that these broaches, rings, and other trinkets would be the identifying factors for family members coming to search through the rows of coffins.

This was a wise strategy, for when the Misery Lane morgue was opened to the public at midnight, many of the bodies were only able to be claimed because of distinguishing possessions, such as an engagement ring or even a gold tooth. One woman was recognized because of the darn her mother had recently made in her stockings, and another was given a name because of a special repair done only the week before to the heel of her shoe.

Walsh had done his best to have the bodies arranged so that the worst cases were farthest from the entrance point. No need to disturb people at the first moment they entered. However, as people neared the end of the rows the emotions swelled considerably. Screaming and wailing were heard constantly, and many people fainted. One woman was so distraught at finding the remains of her daughter that she ran screaming from the morgue and tried to jump into the East River to drown herself. Guards were put up after that to prevent any more suicide attempts.

It is estimated that from the time the morgue opened at Misery Lane until 7:00 Sunday evening about one hundred people per minute viewed the bodies. Nearly 200,000 people stood in line, and more than half of them got in. While many of those who waited their turn had been legitimately looking for relatives (and some returned more than once), there were many thrill seekers in line as well. The grisly scene drew the eyes of those who dared themselves and each other to withstand the horrific sight. Food vendors began setting up

A crowd waits to identify bodies outside the Misery Lane morgue.
(Library of Congress)

in the streets, as though the long line were a parade; others began hawking fake relics from the fire. After many hours of watching nervously giggling young couples and gossiping upper-class socialites wheedle their way into the morgue for intentional chills, Deputy Police Commissioner Driscoll had enough of it. He shouted: "Good God! Do these people imagine that this the Eden Musee? This doesn't go on another minute!"

The crowd was screened more carefully from that point forward, and anyone who did not have a specific person that they were looking for was removed from the line. In addition, Driscoll stationed a nurse named Mary Gray at the front entrance to the morgue. She had a wonderful sense of detecting sincerity and was able to discern the difference between true grieving people and those who were just trying to sneak in for a peak. Now that the crowd was being so closely monitored, the police were also able to apprehend forty known pickpockets who were probably in line with aims of stealing valuables from the coffins and from the people in line around them.

By Sunday night only eighty-eight bodies remained at Misery Lane. Thirty-three of these had been identified but not yet taken to mortuaries. Driscoll ordered the derelicts to carry all these coffins one-hundred feet south of the pier to the real morgue, and he shut down operations at Misery Lane. Another team swept in at midnight to disinfect and fumigate the pier.

On Monday the crowd had thinned somewhat as many in the city returned to their jobs. The weather had also turned cold and rainy. But those who were determined to find their loved ones persisted and waited.

A grief-stricken woman is supported by others after viewing the dead. *(Courtesy of New York Public Library)*

A line of people viewing the bodies at the morgue *(Courtesy of Hulton Archive/Getty Images)*

Many families returned to the lines again and again. Some struggles broke out as coffins were closed up and lifted into hearses because family members were certain that a body that had been identified by someone else belonged to them. At the end of that day there were still twenty-eight unclaimed bodies.

Wednesday night, March 30, sixteen-year-old Sarah Kupla died at St. Vincent's Hospital from the wounds she'd received from falling. She was the last fatality of the fire and the last to have a name and a family to claim her. By the following Saturday night all but seven of the bodies had been identified, and those bodies would never receive names.

Throughout the week, black hearses drawn by horses had arrived to take the claimed bodies away. The crowd outside would become still, silent, and respectful as the flower-adorned carriages went by. Individual funerals took place each day for the victims, attended by friends and family members. The Local 25 relief committee offered some financial assistance to families that were burying a member of the union. By weeks' end, however, it was clear that no one would be giving a funeral to those final seven unknown bodies, and the public was demanding some kind of commemorative event for all who had perished.

On March 29, a committee of the Women's Trade Union League, together with members of Local 25 agreed upon a public funeral and what the rules would be for displaying banners or signs of protest at the event. It was to be a solemn occasion, and any kind of statement would be made with taste and decorum. In the end it was agreed that only union banners could be on hand, and they would need to be draped in black material.

Charities Commissioner Walter Drummond and Mayor William Gaynor announced on that same afternoon that a large plot in the Evergreen Cemetery in Brooklyn would be reserved for the seven unidentified bodies. On April 5, they would be put to rest. In response to this news, the League and Local 25 committee members began to organize their funeral parade to take place on that same day.

Estimates of 400,000 people viewed the parade that day, with more than a third of that number participating in it. Essentially, the parade consisted of two main groups; one met uptown and one met downtown, then both came together at Washington Square. Both arms of the parade began their walk at 1:30 p.m. under a constant downpour of rain following empty hearses, symbolizing all who had died. Those

Union members stand with banners during the Union funeral parade.
(Courtesy of AP Images)

parading were eerily silent as they plodded along through the rain. Only coming within sight of the Asch Building brought out the anguished wails that had been bottled up all afternoon.

It was not all about grief. The League and Local 25 knew that this parade had more significance than just allowing people to mourn. Their purpose in organizing this parade was not lost on journalist Martha Bensley Bruere of *Life and Labor* magazine. She wrote:

> And still as I write the mourning procession moves past in the rain. For two hours they have been going steadily by and the end is not yet in sight. There have been no carriages, no imposing marshals on horseback; just thousands and thousands of working men and women carrying the banners of their trades through the long three-mile tramp in the rain. Never have I seen a military pageant or triumphant ovation so impressive; for it is not because 146 workers were killed in the Triangle shop—not altogether. It is because every year there are 50,000 working men and women killed in the United States—136 a day; almost as many as happened to be killed together on the 25th of March; and because slowly, very slowly, it is dawning on these thousands on thousands that such things do not have to be!

At the same time another large crowd gathered at the morgue to be part of the funeral procession to Evergreen Cemetery. They lined the streets from Misery Lane to the Twenty-third Street Ferry. Starting just after 3:00 that afternoon, the hearses laden with the seven silver coffins began their passage to their final resting place. A carriage filled with flowers and a contingent of city officials, including Commissioner Drummond, followed the hearses. At the ferryboat, close to a hundred mourners rushed aboard just before it lowered its gates and started across the East River to Brooklyn. Among the passengers was Carrie Lefkowitz, who said, "I have lost my sister, Minnie Mayer. Every day, since the fire, I visited the morgue. Every day, I peered into those poor burned faces but my sister I cannot tell. I feel that

Horses draped in black pull coffins during a funeral procession for the unidentified victims of the fire. *(Library of Congress)*

one of those in the wagons is my sister. So I follow them to the cemetery."

In the months that followed, several newspapers kept close account of what happened in the aftermath of the fire; the *World* and the *New York Times* were foremost among them. Short obituaries and vignettes of no more than a paragraph ran about the victims and survivors in the papers for days after the fire, more appearing with each family member found alive or corpse identified. The entire Lower East Side was affected. There seemed to be a fatality for every block in that section of the city; everyone living in the tenements knew someone who had perished.

A few of the stories had happy endings such as finding loved ones or friends still alive after having lost track of each other in the rush to escape. Yet even those who lived through the fire and made it home would be haunted for the rest of their lives by memories. "We didn't sleep right, always afraid," said Pauline Cuoio Pepe. "We were also angry. 'What the hell did they close the door for? What did they think we're going out with? What are we gonna do, steal a shirtwaist? Who the heck wanted a shirtwaist?'"

seven
The Trial

Someone had to be at fault. Someone had to be punished. That was the general feeling throughout the city in the first few weeks after the fire. While the newspapers continued to put stories about the fire on the front pages, New York citizens continued to rage about injustice and ineptness. William Randolph Hearst, a newspaper publisher, was more eager than most to keep stories of this event and its aftermath in his press. He took a hard line against the city officials that allowed the Asch Building to pass fire safety codes when, in his opinion, it was clearly incapable of withstanding a fire. He especially pointed his fingers at the owners of the Triangle Factory for being criminally negligent, and many of his readers agreed with him.

District Attorney Charles Whitman also believed that Harris and Blanck needed to be taken to task for the deaths of so many of their employees. It wasn't just that they were the

William Randolph Hearst *(Library of Congress)*

bosses and should be held responsible. He strongly believed that the door to the Washington Place stairwell exit had been locked on the ninth floor at closing time by orders from the Triangle owners to prevent theft. While an initial investigation of the scene had Fire Marshal Edward Beers claiming that there appeared to be no doors locked and that many of the victims on the ninth floor died where they stood from the sheer heat of the fire, Charles Whitman didn't accept that finding. Too many bodies had been found near that ninth-floor door, and too many survivors related stories of how they couldn't get out that way.

On April 10, Charles Whitman and his team of assistants brought their evidence against Harris and Blanck to court

Charles Whitman *(Library of Congress)*

to get an indictment. An indictment happens when a judge and a grand jury agree that prosecutors have enough testimony and hard evidence to prove that a suspected criminal should be arrested and go to trial. Whitman had plenty of testimony. All day long, he questioned survivors of the fire about how they escaped from the building, what the conditions and rules of the workplace had been, and what happened to friends or relatives they knew who hadn't survived. His main intention was to show the grand jury two reasons that Harris and Blanck were responsible for the deaths of so many Triangle workers. One: Harris and Blanck knew that the ninth-floor door to the Washington Place stairwell was locked at the time of the fire and, in fact, had ordered it to be that way; and two: because they purposely kept the lofts full of such large amounts of combustible material by not having it removed promptly, they were responsible for the magnitude and speed of the fire.

Still, they had no hard evidence, something jurors could put in their hands to prove guilt. The Ninth Street door had burned up along with all the cloth. Whitman knew he could win if only he had the actual lock from the door, so he sent a new team of investigators that afternoon to search through the ninth floor of the Asch Building again. They were to focus specifically on the area around that ninth-floor Washington Place stairwell doorway. It had been fifteen days since the fire and several investigations had already been completed of the site. Many doubted anything of value would be found if it hadn't been discovered already. Yet Whitman's small hired team succeeded that afternoon when digging into the rubbish and embers around the door. There, under a pile of debris was the lock to the door, completely intact, with the

This political cartoon depicts a greedy businessman holding the door
of the factory as the trapped workers inside burn.

bolt sticking out as it would have been if locked. The coloring of the lock also showed how it must have been locked during the fire, for the bolt was not damaged by the heat in any way.

This door lock was brought into evidence on April 11, and the grand jury immediately ordered the indictment. That same afternoon Blanck and Harris were arrested. Keeping the door locked during business hours was only a misdemeanor, but because breaking that law lead to the deaths of people under their employ, it became much more serious. Their crime was manslaughter, punishable by a twenty-year jail sentence. Technically, they were only arraigned for the deaths of two people out of all 146 that perished. The punishment was the same if they were tried for one death or all of them, so to make the case more clear-cut, the prosecutors narrowed it down to the two victims they felt they could prove without a doubt died because of the orders of the Triangle owners. Between the indictment and the actual trial, the case was refocused to be about one woman only, a seamstress named Margaret Schwartz who died on the ninth floor of the Asch Building.

The "Shirtwaist Kings" were brought before the court on April 12 and then released on $25,000 bail. They hired the best defense lawyer in New York, a man named Max Steuer, who had never lost a case. Through his efforts to jam up the system with appeals, the actual trial was pushed all the way to December, eight months after the fire.

Serving as prosecutor was Charles Bostwick. Judge Thomas C. T. Crain presided over the case. Jury selection began on December 4, 1911, and the testimony began two days later. Hundreds of mourners packed the hallways of the

Charles Bostwick (far right) stands with investigators on the roof of the Asch Building.

courthouse, slinging accusations at Harris, Blanck, and their attorney as they entered the building and made their way to the courtroom. It was a highly emotional scene, but Steuer had directed his clients to keep their profiles low and let the scathing remarks pass by without incident.

The big issue in the case was the definition of reasonable doubt. Bostwick had to prove that Harris and Blanck were responsible for the death of Margaret Schwartz beyond a reasonable doubt. In other words, the jury needed to be certain that Harris and Blanck were guilty and not have any feelings that questions had been left unanswered or proof was lacking substance. Bostwick had only eyewitness testimony and a lock to share with the jury. With this scant evidence he had to convince the jury that his witnesses were honest and that their stories were valid. Steuer knew this and did everything in his power to create holes in the stories of the witnesses and make their tales sound trumped up, rehearsed, or invented.

Steuer made his biggest impact on the jurors in the way he interrogated the teenaged, immigrant witnesses. He made a point of uncovering the weaknesses in their skill at speaking English. When a witness said something that seemed to be a poor word choice, he made sure to repeat it as a question and then have them say it again in the same way to accent the mistake. This had the effect of making the witnesses sound less intelligent and therefore less believable.

The testimony of Kate Alterman, one the prosecution's key witnesses who had actually seen Margaret Schwartz catch on fire, got completely turned around and was made to seem ridiculous during Steuer's inquisition. Her testimony sounded too rehearsed, as she used many descriptive terms in her story such as describing one worker as jumping around "like a wildcat" and the fire being like "a red curtain of flame." Steuer started his questioning with easy to answer inquiries about how she had moved to Philadelphia to be with her family after the fire and had been brought back for the trial. After she had relaxed some he asked her, "Now I want you to tell me your story over again, *just as you told it before*." Thinking she needed to repeat not just the point of the story but also her actual wording of it, Alterman did her best to retell the details in the same exact phrasing. As he had hoped, Steuer succeeded at making her story come across as something she was taught to say in a specific, dramatic way. It appeared to be rehearsed. Steuer had her do this several more times before he was done with her.

Bostwick tried to save the situation during redress by asking her ". . . each time that you have answered Mr. Steuer's question you have tried to repeat it in the same language that you first told it here in court, have you not?" But it was too late to repair the damage done by her testimony. Her story came across as a lie, and it was only made worse when he asked her to try to tell the story as she had originally told it before the indictment back in April. She could not remember the words she had used so many months ago and was too befuddled to be of use to the case anymore.

The battle between the lawyers was hard, with Bostwick edging ahead with a great bit of testimony and Steuer finding every conceivable way to make it unreliable. Even when it came to the hard evidence of the door lock, Steuer found ways to make the jury doubt its validity. He suggested through his witnesses, such as Fire Captain Howard Ruch, that the district attorney's detectives had to have planted the lock, because no one else had seen it during their previous investigations. Steuer told the court:

> Hundreds upon hundreds of people go into that debris and seek the bodies, and the Fire Department makes a conclusive and minute and detailed search into that debris, and the whole question that is being agitated in the press day after day is locks, locks, locks, Your Honor. And nothing is found. When on the tenth of April, as from a clear sky, a detective goes to the premises and . . . within twenty-five minutes a lock is discovered.

Bostwick, desperate to keep the lock as valid evidence had expert witnesses, people who testify about a particular subject in relation to a trial rather than as witnesses to the crime, come and identify the lock and how it was used. John D. Moore, a consultant engineer hired by the district attorney tried to explain under oath how the lock had to have been from the ninth floor Washington Place door: "The hinges [on the door] were on the right hand side; that is to say, if you stood inside the Washington Place loft, the hinges would have been on the side to the right. That is to say, if you were facing the door on the inside of the loft the handle to the door, if it had one, would be on your left hand. Now a door which moved in that direction is known as a left-handed door."

But Steuer turned right around and used Bostwick's experts against him. Francis J. Kelly, an employee of Reading Hardware, had originally been hired by Bostwick to testify about filling the order for this lock and install-ing it on the door—his purpose was to identify the lock. However, under Steuer's cross-examination, he had to admit that the locks were neither left nor right-handed; they could be used either way. So, this particular lock was proved to be no longer unique and it sat in evidence with no power or influence over the jury.

And although Bostwick had a parade of fire survivors tell how they couldn't exit the building because the door was always locked during business hours, Steuer managed to find plenty of his own witnesses who told how they went through that door all the time during business hours and even found two women who claimed to have opened the door during the fire but didn't escape that way because they thought the stairwell was on fire.

Bostwick succeeded at showing the Triangle Company owners to be cheap and petty. In defending why they kept the doors locked and a security guard posted, Harris told of a time in 1908 when there was a rash of shirtwaist thefts by employees. However, Bostwick managed to coax out of Harris that the value of all the good stolen in one year: "Well," Harris confessed, "ten dollars or fifteen dollars or twelve dollars or eight dollars, something like that."

Yet, despite all that, Steuer still managed to make Harris and Blanck look sympathetic against all of Bostwick's character damaging questions. The owners were, after all, survivors of the fire, too. They had relatives who worked for them in the building that day. Harris had a sister who narrowly survived on the eighth floor. Samuel Bernstein, the floor manager, was their cousin, and his brother died on the ninth floor. Didn't Harris play a big hand in saving the lives of his tenth-floor employees by acting quickly and rationally? To the eyes of the jury, all businessmen themselves, the Triangle owners appeared to have been as much victims of this fire as any of the poor immigrants that had already spoken against them.

It didn't help Bostwick that the shock of the many gruesome deaths attributed to the fire couldn't be used as an effective tool in the trial. He had hoped to tug on the emotions of the jury by having Triangle fire survivors talk about how their loved ones perished, but Judge Crain quickly forbid any talk of the fire outside of the details pertaining to the specifics of the case. He did not allow any discussion of the fire escape, jumping from the building, or any other graphic subjects.

So, when it came down to the final statements, both lawyers pounced on the topic of doubt by focusing on who had told the truth and who had perjured themselves. What would motivate a witness to lie? Steuer made good points about why Bernstein and the other Triangle employees would be unlikely to lie about stories that helped to defend their bosses: they were still on the payroll; they had relatives who had died; they were suing the owners for damages. In other words, they had no reason to protect Harris and Blanck. Bostwick pointed out that his witnesses were young, hardworking girls who needed their employment. They spoke from the heart and out of mourning. "Gentlemen, believe this testimony," he said to the jury in his closing statement, "believe the testimony of those honest little girls that were here, and that told their stories from their hearts, believe them, as you must, and one of the most awful and greatest crimes of history has been proven and it not to be punished in this Court."

But none of Bostwick's claims could compete against these simple statements from Steuer's closing remarks:

> Beyond a reasonable doubt, did the People prove that Harris and Blanck killed Margaret Schwartz through the negligent way they conducted their business? Beyond a reasonable doubt did the People prove not only that door was locked, because that is of no consequence, did they prove beyond a reasonable doubt that Margaret Schwartz died because that door was locked? Did they prove that that door was locked? Did they prove anything against these defendants?

Just before three o'clock on December 27, after hearing 155 witnesses testify over twenty-three days, the jury retired to deliberate. Their orders were specific from Judge Crain. He told them they could only convict Harris and Blanck if the prosecution had proved that the door was locked, if the

Triangle owners knew it was locked, and that being locked it caused the death of Margaret Schwartz. Any doubt of those facts made the owners innocent. It took only one hour and fifty minutes for them to decide.

At 4:45 p.m., the jury declared Isaac Harris and Max Blanck not guilty.

eight
From the Ashes

The people of New York wanted to blame someone for the deaths of the Triangle workers. While a lot of focus went specifically to the Triangle Company owners, heat was put on other people as well. Specifically, the unions, Tammany Hall, the legislature, and the governor were targets of protesters wanting to know why this fire hadn't been prevented and what would stop another fire just like it from happening again.

Within a week of the fire, meetings had been held by eight different organizations to sort out who had been responsible for the fire. That Wednesday, the International Ladies Garment Workers Union held a memorial meeting at Grand Central Palace in which thousands of people attended, but it was too soon after the event for any real discussion to take place. Women became hysterical with grief, some fainting, others wailing and screaming. It took sixty policemen to help the bereaved women out the doors and restore some peace to the event. Those who remained heard a passionate plea to unionize all garment workers.

Another emotional crowd gathered on Friday night at Cooper Union, the same place where the vote to strike in 1909 was decided, to remember the victims. At that event, Methodist preacher Dr. Anna Shaw, an important suffragist leader, said what many people in the city were thinking, "As I read the terrible story of the fire I asked, am I my sister's keeper?'. . . And I bowed my head and said, 'I am responsible.' Yes, every man and woman in this city is responsible. Don't try to lay it on someone else. Don't try to lay it on some official."

It was a fact that no one in the city could deny. They liked being able to buy their clothing at inexpensive prices, and to do so they turned blind eyes to the desperate conditions of the workers who toiled in the factories. No one had spoken up or demanded change until now. She took the opportunity to add her own agenda regarding women's suffrage, and how if women had the right to add their vote, things might be different. "You men—forget not that you are responsible! As voters it was your business and you should have been about your business. If you are incompetent, then in the name of Heaven stand aside and let us try!"

This same concept was brought home again on Sunday night, April 2, 1911, one week and a day after the fire. A public meeting was held at the Metropolitan Opera House, featuring a panel of distinguished speakers. Among them was a petite twenty-nine-year-old woman named Rose Schneiderman, a speaker for the Women's Trade Union League. She had played a major role in helping the strike of 1909 by gathering funding and motivating the workers. On this night, she said:

> I would be a traitor to those poor burned bodies if I were to come here and talk good fellowship We have tried you good people of the public—and we have found you wanting. . . . This is not the first time girls have been burned alive in the city. Every week I must learn of the untimely death of one of my sister workers. Every year thousands of us are maimed. The life of men and women is so cheap and property is so sacred. There are so many of us for one job it matters little if 146 of us are burned to death.

The speech roused those in attendance into action. For many, the call was to help support the families of the victims. Aid for both the injured survivors and those who had lost relatives came from a variety of sources. Donations poured in from the public at large, but the larger sums came from prominent figures in New York City. Theater owner Marcus Loew gave proceeds of his Broadway productions, while Lee and J. J. Shubert used their theater to do a benefit performance. Movie producer William Fox donated proceeds from showings at his movie house. William Carnegie, the philanthropic millionaire, donated money. Many others came forward with help, too, and $120,000 was contributed overall.

The Red Cross began their work in assisting the needy families as early as Monday morning, March 27, but few came forward asking for help. These Italian and Jewish families were used to hard lives and taking care of themselves. They didn't think to ask for charity because of their pride and grief. As the donations came in, Red Cross workers had to go the tenement neighborhoods to find the needy and bring aid to them directly. Some money had to be shipped overseas to families back in Europe who depended on the money sent home that would not be coming anymore. Many of the far-away families learned about the deaths of their daughters and sisters in the same letter that contained relief money.

Yet while relief was a strong area of concern for the masses of New York, something people felt they could directly effect, there were others at the Metropolitan Opera House who had heard Schneiderman speak and felt a different stirring. For them, the drive became to effect change and to assure that a tragedy of this kind would never happen again.

Among these fighters was a woman named Frances Perkins. She was a progressive suffragist born into money, with a master's degree in social science from Columbia University. Her passion was studying the downtrodden, gathering facts, and then using those facts to enact change. She had worked as a lobbyist to help pass a bill that would limit the number of hours a person had to work to fifty-four per week.

Perkins worked with and was known by the people involved in Tammany Hall. Tammany Hall was an organization that had been started in 1786 as a brotherhood of rich men who wanted to use their influence to help the poor and destitute. As time passed, the group gained a steady influence amongst the working class and immigrants, and their focus shifted away from social reform and towards political manipulation. Tammany Hall representatives literally approached immigrants as they got off the boats, helping them find jobs and lodgings in exchange for the new citizens voting for Tammany Hall candidates. Combining this with a system called bossism, in which Tammany Hall bosses

Rose Schneiderman (pictured here) gave a rousing speech at a public meeting held at the Metropolitan Opera House, prompting an influx of aid for the fire victims and their families. *(Library of Congress)*

controlled different territories, the organization became a dominant and nearly unstoppable political machine. Though frequently corrupt, it was nearly impossible to get anything done without Tammany Hall's support, and Frances Perkins was known and liked by the Tammany Hall bosses.

Before the speech on April 2, Perkins had never met Rose Schneiderman, but the words the young redhead spoke moved her deeply. She had also been a witness to the fire from the street, and the images from it were still vivid in her mind. Right after the opera house meeting a Committee on Safety was formed, with her volunteering as the lobbyist.

Perkins and the committee took their cause to Albany, the state capitol, but the governor was not interested in helping. Next she went to the legislature, to speak to Al Smith, assembly member for the Eastside district. In a speech Perkins gave years later, she recounted some valuable advice he gave her:

> You're going to form a commission, that's all right, that's a good idea, but let me tell you. Don't get started asking the governor to appoint a commission . . . If you want to get anything done, you got to have this, a legislative commission. If the legislature does it, the legislature will be proud of it, the legislature will listen to their report and the legislature will do something about it. But if the governor appoints the commission, they will just give it the cold shoulder; they won't pay any attention to it."

So following Smith's advice, Perkins began working to set up a legislative commission. Smith decided to include himself as part of the commission, and he teamed up with Senator Robert Wagner to get it put together. Thanks to their support, on June 30, 1911, Governor Dix put his signature on the law that made the Factory Investigating Committee

Frances Perkins *(Library of Congress)*

a reality. To represent the governor, two citizens were put on the committee; one was Mary Dreier, the WTUL president. The governor also appointed Abram Elkus to work as council for the committee without fee.

Frances Perkins, of course, was part of the committee, or as she put it, "I was a young person then and certainly not fit for service on any super commission but I was the chief—I was the investigator, and in charge of the investigations and this was an extraordinary opportunity, you see, to get into factories to make a report and be sure it was going to be heard." Perkins arranged a group of investigators to work with her, including Rose Schneiderman. Smith asked Dr. George Price from the Joint Board of Sanitary Control to help investigate also, and he led a team into roughly 2,000 factories throughout New York state in that first year of the committee's existence.

The committee was initially only given $10,000 to use for its investigations, and the scope of its research was primarily aimed at fire safety. However, the scope quickly widened to include all safety hazards in the workplace such as poor sanitation or ventilation, cleanliness, and dangers posed by machinery. It also looked closely at how the employees were treated. Were they working too many long hours; were there enough breaks; were they paid enough; were children being used for labor; and was work being sent home with employees? Committee members volunteered their time and used the money to pay for operations. Every Saturday, Perkins reported her findings at a public hearing either before the governor or just the committee for four years.

In October 1911, the committee did a public hearing specifically addressing the Triangle Factory Fire. Several fire chiefs who had been on the scene during the fire and building inspectors were called in to testify. All of them agreed that while the Asch Building itself was fireproof, the contents within it were highly flammable. Also, the structure didn't provide adequate exits for the tenants of the buildings because the fire escape was weak and ended abruptly above a closed courtyard, and the exit doors to the stairwells opened inward instead of out.

But it was the testimony of Fire Chief Edward Croker that was the most telling. Two months before the trial of Harris and Blanck, he pointed blame in more directions than just the head partners of the Triangle Company.

> The Asch Building fire started with the Fire Department. The Fire Department says, "Our records are all right; everything we ordered was complied with." The Building Department says, "Our records are all right." The Health Department says, "Our records are all right." The Police Department have not got through investigating yet, and I don't think they ever will and nobody is responsible. There are just as many factories in New York in the same condition as the Asch Building was and probably is today.

The committee agreed and continued its efforts to ensure that responsibility be taken by someone.

By the end of 1912 the New York Factory Investigation Committee had looked into businesses in forty-five cities, some of the worst places visited by Smith and Wagner themselves. This work amounted to eight new laws being created for labor code conditions. In 1913 the influence of Tammany Hall helped the committee push twenty-five more bills through the legislature, creating new laws that were unprecedented in United State history for industrial reform. The following year another three bills passed as laws. This period of time is often referred to as the golden era in remedial factory legislation.

Every one of the problems with the Asch building was addressed in these new laws. A fire like that of the Triangle Factory shouldn't happen again.

Yet it did.

In 1958, author Leon Stein, the first man to write a comprehensive account of the Triangle Factory Fire, received a call from a friend who happened to be one of the survivors of the Triangle fire. She screamed over the wire that a building was on fire in the city and that the factory workers were trapped and jumping out the windows. In all the years that had passed, and for all the laws created, sweatshop conditions still existed then. And they still exist now. Most of them are in foreign countries now, but there are still some in the larger cities of America, such as Los Angeles and New York, that take advantage of illegal immigrants or new legal immigrants, by making them work in unsafe conditions for less than minimum wage. It is an illegal practice here in America, but the problem continues to be a concern.

Isaac Harris and Max Blanck certainly didn't learn their lesson from the trial of 1911. They went out and opened a new factory and committed the same crime of locking the employees inside. Blanck was brought to trial twice more for this offense, and both times he claimed to be trying to find a lock that would satisfy both his need to prevent theft and yet comply with the law as being a lock that was easily undone. At one of the hearings the judge knew he must punish Blanck for breaking the law but ordered the smallest penalty possible: a fine of $20. Lawsuits from victims of the fire continued to plague the Triangle owners for three years after the fire. Despite the huge sum they were rewarded by their insurance company (an amount well above the actual damages), they finally settled twenty-three suits in court in 1914, only having to pay $75 per life lost in the fire.

Harris quit the business of trying to run a factory with Blanck in 1920 and returned to the quieter life of being a tailor. Blanck continued trying to operate shirtwaist companies under a variety of names but went out of business sometime before 1925 when his name ceased to be in public business records.

In 1918 Al Smith became governor of New York and was very popular. He eventually ran for president of the United Sates but lost to Herbert Hoover. Frances Perkins continued to work alongside Smith when he was governor; he appointed her to the New York State Industrial Commission. She had the honor of being the highest paid state employee in the entire country through that position. When Democrat Franklin D. Roosevelt became president of the United States, he hired her as secretary of labor; she was the first woman to serve on the cabinet. When he created the New Deal, a plan of action to help pull the country out of the Great Depression, Perkins was essential in implementing his plans, and she stayed on the cabinet for his entire four terms in office.

Rose Schneiderman took over as president of the WTUL after Mary Dreier left, doing great work alongside her friend Eleanor Roosevelt. In 1937 President Roosevelt hired Schneiderman onto his staff as the only woman commissioner of the National Recovery Administration. After her term with the president, she returned home to become the secretary of labor for New York. Robert Wagner continued to serve in the Senate throughout Roosevelt's entire presidency and was also an invaluable help to the president's work.

Fifty years after the fire, the ILGWU honored the anniversary of the fire, and the memory of those lost, by having a plaque installed on the building that once housed the Triangle Shirtwaist Company at the corner of Washington Place and Greene Street. On March 25, 2003, Mayor Michael Bloomberg of New York City presided over another honorific event at the same site of the fire. The Asch Building, now called the Brown Building, still stands in a part of New York City known as Greenwich Village and houses classrooms for New York University. On that Tuesday morning the ten-story building was dedicated as a National Landmark. As a bronze plaque was unveiled to commemorate the building's place in history, Bloomberg said, "It was one of the worst industrial disasters, not just in New York City's history but really in the history of the whole country. It was horrific and worst of all it was largely preventable." Bloomberg went on to say in a more positive tone, "The land marking of the Triangle Shirtwaist Factory site serves to remind us about one of our greatest assets: New York's ability to follow great tragedy with great progress." Indeed, this workplace fire spurred great progress for the entire nation in the area of industry reform.

And on that spring morning, a list of every victim of the fire was read aloud. A bell chimed solemnly after each name. Those in attendance reverently placed white carnations on the sidewalk in remembrance of each person lost so long ago.

Timeline

1900
Isaac Harris and Max Blanck open Triangle
Waist Company on Wooster Street.

1901
Asch Building constructed.

1902
Triangle Waist Company moves into top three
floors of Asch Building.

1903
The Women's Trade Union League is formed.

1906
Ladies Waist Makers Union absorbed into
International League of Garment Workers
Union, Local 25.

1908
Jacob Kline leads Triangle employees in walkout.

1909
SEPTEMBER   Triangle workers go on strike.
NOVEMBER 23   20,000 shirtwaist workers join Triangle
employees on strike.

1910
FEBRUARY 8   Strike comes to an end.

1911
MARCH 25   Fire breaks out at Triangle Waist Factory
at 4:45 p.m.

MARCH 26	200,000 people line up to identify and view the fire victims at Misery Lane.
MARCH 29	Last victim of fire dies.
APRIL 5	Citywide memorial event takes place.
APRIL 11	Isaac Harris and Max Blanck indicted for manslaughter.
JUNE 30	Factory Investigating Committee bill signed by Governor Dix of New York.
OCTOBER	Factory Investigating Committee leads public hearing about Triangle Factory fire.
DECEMBER 4	Trial begins for Harris and Blanck.
DECEMBER 27	Case against Harris and Blanck dismissed.

1912
Eight new workplace safety laws created.

1913
Twenty-five new workplace safety laws created.

1914
Lawsuits from victims against Harris and Blanck settled.

1961
International League of Garment Workers Union has memorial plaque attached to Asch Building.

MARCH 25

2003
Site of Triangle Factory Fire becomes national landmark.

Sources

CHAPTER ONE: Fire at the Factory

p. 9, "the city might have a fire . . ." Leon Stein, *The Triangle Fire* (Ithaca and London: ILR/Cornell University Press, 1962), 27.

p. 12, "Limited to the air . . ." *New York, A Documentary Film: The Power and the People, Episode Four, 1898-1918* (Steeple Chase Films, 1999).

p. 16, "She appeared in a stiff shirtwaist . . ." "The History of the Herald Square Hotel: Charles Dana Gibson and the Gibson Girls," http://www.heraldsquarehotel.com.

p. 19, "The last time I removed the rags . . ." Stein, *The Triangle Fire,* 33.

CHAPTER TWO: New Yorkers

p. 25, "Going to America . . ." Nancy Foner, *From Ellis Island to JFK*, (New York: Russell Sage Foundation, Yale University Press, 2000), 23.

p. 26, "Were we snobby!" Jeff Kisseloff, *You Must Remember This: An Oral History of Manhattan from the 1890s to World War II* (New York: Harcourt Brace Jovanovich, Publishers, 1989), 96.

p. 29, "I laid out the factory . . ." David Von Drehle, *Triangle: The Fire that Changed America* (New York: Grove Press, 2003), 44.

p. 30, "I went to work . . ." Kisseloff, *You Must Remember This*, 34.

CHAPTER THREE: Shirtwaist Workers Strike

p. 31-32, "The committee here . . ." "Sweatshops in America," Smithsonian Institution's National Museum of American History and Office of Exhibit Center, http://americanhistory.si.edu/sweatshops/intro/intro.htm.

p. 33, "An unscrupulous character . . ." Ibid.

p. 33, "A God-given right to light . . ." George J. Lankevich, *American Metropolis: A History of New York City* (New York: New York University Press, 1998), 128.

p. 37, "assist in the organization . . ." Von Drehle, *Triangle: The Fire that Changed America*, 15.

p. 38, "Will you stay at your machines . . ." Ibid., 36.

p. 41, "There comes a time . . ." Ibid., 56.

p. 42, "I want to say . . . general strike," Ibid., 56-57.

CHAPTER FOUR: Fire from the Outside

p. 50-51, "The crowds were jamming . . ." "Stories of Survivors and Witnesses and Rescuers Outside Tell What They Saw," *New York Times*, March 26, 1911.

p. 51, "a bale of dark dress goods," Stein, *The Triangle Fire*, 14.

p. 52, "It looked like a parcel . . ." "From the Charles Willis Thompson Letters, Rare and Manuscript Collections," Cornell University Library, Ithaca, NY, The Triangle Factory Fire, http://www.ilr.cornell.edu/trianglefire/texts/letters/dearwm_letter.html?location=.

p. 52, "The screams brought me running," Stein, *The Triangle Fire*, 14.

p. 52, "My God, the people couldn't get out . . ." Kisselhoff, *You Must Remember This*, 34.

p. 52-53, "I was upstairs in our . . ." "Stories of Survivors And Witnesses and Rescuers Outside Tell What They Saw."

p. 54, "We had to lift them off . . ." Stein, *The Triangle Fire*, 17.

p. 54, "It would be impossible . . . hit the sidewalk," "Testimony of Fire Chief Edward F. Croker At First Public Hearing," October 10, 1911, Kheel Center for Labor

Management Documentation and Archives, Cornell
University, Ithaca, NY, http://www.ilr.cornell.
edu/trianglefire/texts.

p. 54-55, "What good were life nets?" Stein, *The Triangle
Fire*, 17.

p. 58, "The floods of water . . ." Leon Stein, *Out of the
Sweatshop: The Struggle for Industrial Democracy*
(New York: Quadrangle/New Times Book Company,
1977), 188-193.

CHAPTER FIVE: The Fire Inside

p. 62, "The fire was running away . . ." Von Drehle.
Triangle: The Fire that Changed America, 122.

p. 63, "Try to get the girls out . . ." Ibid., 123.

p. 63, "I just drove them out," Ibid.

p. 63, "I had to push the girls . . ." Stein, *The Triangle
Fire*, 39.

p. 65, "I can't get anyone!" Ibid., 40.

p. 70-71, "When I first opened . . . all around them," Von
Drehle, *Triangle: The Fire that Changed America,* 150.

p. 71, "I could not make out . . ." Ibid., 146.

p. 72, "A body struck the top . . ." Stein, *The Triangle
Fire*, 66.

CHAPTER SIX: Claiming the Dead

p. 78, "I had a lot . . ." Kisseloff, *You Must Remember
This,* 34-35.

p. 78-79, "I remember how with my last . . ." Stein, *The
Triangle Fire*, 72.

p. 82, "My men and I . . ." Ibid., 85.

p. 84, "Good God!" Ibid., 103.

p. 89, "And still as I write . . ." Stein, *Out of the Sweatshop:
The Struggle for Industrial Democracy,* 194-195.

p. 90-91, "I have lost my sister..." Stein, *The Triangle Fire*, 153-154.

p. 91, "We didn't sleep . . ." Kisseloff, *You Must Remember This,* 35.

CHAPTER SEVEN: The Trial

p. 99, "like a wildcat . . . " "Testimony of Miss Kate Alterman," Excerpts from Trial Testimony in the Triangle Shirtwaist Fire Trial, University of Missouri-Kansas City School of Law, Kansas City, MO, http://www.law.umkc.edu/faculty/projects/ftrials/triangle/triangletest1.html.

p. 99, "Now I want you to tell me . . . " Ibid.

p. 100, "each time you have answered . . . " Ibid.

p. 100, "Hundreds upon hundreds . . ." Von Drehle, *Triangle: The Fire that Changed America,* 239-240.

p. 101, "The hinges [on the door] . . ." "John D. Moore," Excerpts from Trial Testimony in the Triangle Shirtwaist Fire Trial, University of Missouri-Kansas City School of Law, Kansas City, MO,http://www.law.umkc.edu/faculty/projects/ftrials/triangle/triangletest1.html.

p. 102, "Well, ten dollars or fifteen..." VonDrehle, *Triangle: The Fire that Changed America,* 253.

p. 103, "Gentlemen, believe this testimony . . ." "Summation of Charles Bostwick for the Prosecution in the Triangle Shirtwaist Fire Trial," University of Missouri-Kansas City School of Law, Kansas City, MO, http://www.law.umkc.edu/faculty/projects/ftrials/triangle/bostwicksumm.html.

p. 103, "Beyond a reasonable doubt . . . " "Summation of Max D. Steuer for the Defense in the Triangle Shirtwaist Fire Trial," University of Missouri-Kansas City School of Law, Kansas City, MO, http://www.law.umkc.edu/faculty/projects/ftrials/triangle/steuersumm.html.

CHAPTER EIGHT: From the Ashes

p. 106, "As I read . . . let us try!" Stein, *The Triangle Fire*, 139.

p. 107, "I would be a traitor . . ." Rose Schneiderman, "We Have Found You Wanting," Kheel Center for Labor-Management Documentation and Archives, Cornell University, Ithaca, NY, http://www.ilr.cornell. edu/trianglefire/texts/stein_ootss/ootss_rs. html?location=Murning+and+Protest.

p. 110, "You're going to form a commission . . . " Frances Perkins (lecture, Cornell University, School of Industrial and Labor Relations, Ithaca, NY, September 30, 1964), http://www.ilr.cornell.edu/trianglefire/texts/lectures/perkins.html.

p. 111, "I was a young person . . . " Ibid.

p. 113, "The Asch Building fire started . . . " "Fire Chief Edward F. Croker: Key Testimony Before the Fire Investigating Commission Concerning the Triangle Shirtwaist Factory Fire," University of Missouri-Kansas City School of Law, Kansas City, MO,http://www.law. umkc.edu/faculty/projects/ftrials/triangle/commistestim. html.

p. 116, "It was one of the worst . . . " Associated Press, "Site of tragic factory fire name city landmark," *CNN.com*, March 26, 2003, http://www.cnn.com/2003/US/Northeast/03/26/fire.landmark.ap/.

p. 116, "The land marking of the Triangle . . . " Andrea Friedman, "Equity Shows Union Solidarity at Triangle Shirtwaist Factory Landmark Tribute," Actors' Equity Association, March 26, 2003,http://www.actorsequity. org/theatrenews/triangle_03-26-2003.html.

Bibliography

Ewing, Elizabeth. *History of 20th Century Fashion*. London: B. T. Batsford Ltd., 1974.

Foner, Nancy. *From Ellis Island to JFK: New York's Two Great Waves of Immigration*. New Haven and London: Yale University Press, 2000.

Kisseloff, Jeff. *You Must Remember This: An Oral History of Manhattan from the 1890s to World War II*. New York: Harcourt Brace Jovanovich, 1989.

Lankevich, George J. *American Metropolis, A History of New York City*. New York: New York University Press, 1998.

Lieurance, Suzanne. *The Triangle Shirtwaist Fire and Sweatshop Reform*. New Jersey: Enslow Publishers, Inc., 2003.

Milbank, Caroline Rennolds. *New York Fashion: The Evolution of American Style*. New York: Harry N. Abrams, Inc., 1989.

Schoener, Allon. *New York: An Illustrated History of the People*. New York: W.W. Norton & Company, 1998.

Stein, Leon. *Out of the Sweatshop: The Struggle for Industrial Democracy*. New York: Quadrangle/New Times Book Company, 1977.

Stein, Leon. *The Triangle Fire*. Ithaca and London: Cornell University Press, 1990.

VonDrehle, David. *Triangle: The Fire that Changed America*. New York: Grove Press, 2003.

Weatherford, Doris. *American Women's History*. New York: Prentice Hall General Reference, 1994.

White, Norval. *New York, A Physical History*. New York: Atheneum, 1987.

Web Sites

http://www.ilr.cornell.edu/trianglefire
A Web exhibit about the Triangle Fire, created by Cornell University. In addition to summarizing the events, contains links to original documents, articles, and testimony about the fire.

http://www.tenement.org
Web site of the Lower East Side Tenement Museum, in New York City, which is dedicated to documenting urban life in the United States at the end of the nineteenth and beginning of the twentieth century. In addition to information about the museum, there is online information about the time period.

http://www.dol.gov/oasam/programs/history/main.htm
The history section of the U.S. Department of Labor, with information about labor history, and links to government documents about the Triangle Fire and other incidents.

http://www.archives.nysed.gov/aindex.shtml
The homepage of the New York State Archives, containing documents about the fire and other labor issues.

Index